INSIDER TIP The orient in the west

The Moorish past is not just palpable in the Alhambra and Mezquita but also in small oases like the Capilla Mudéjar in the Jewish Quarter in Córdoba → p. 37

INSIDER TIP Mini hotel in Marbella

How to avoid the glittery big hotels in Marbella – try La Morada Más Hermosa, a small hotel with six charming rooms and a lemon tree

INSIDER TIP Beach raci...

The first race on ... Sanlúcar de Barran... more than 160 year... fun and be seen – th... Cabaïlo has everything that a horse-race should have → p. 119

the fortress, ... further down, ...esque narrow ...La Real is the most beautiful place in the Sierra de Aracena → p. 35

INSIDER TIP Great tapas

Granada is the tapas capital. The Taberna La Tana is small, excellent and not in the least touristy. Wide choice of wines by the glass → p. 69

INSIDER TIP Pottery mad

Úbeda is well know for its pottery. Beautiful items can be found in traditionally-run Alfarería Tito, for example → p. 75

INSIDER TIP Royal collection

Isabella's personal collection of 15th-century paintings by Flemish and Italian Old Masters hangs in the Capilla Real in Granada → p. 69

INSIDER TIP Barbecuing in the country

Tucked-away in a shady spot not far from Vejer de la Frontera is the open-air restaurant La Castillería where Juan Valdés demonstrates his culinary and barbecue skills → p. 83

BEST OF ...

GREAT PLACES FOR FREE
Discover new places and save money

● **Baroque at its best**
The 'Siglo de Oro', the 'Golden Age', was a period in which the arts flourished in Spain. Master painters include Diego Velázquez, Francisco de Zurbarán and José de Ribera. The *Museo de Bellas Artes* in Sevilla is free if you have a passport from an EU country→ p. 51

● **The Alhambra in all its glory**
Sitting at the *Mirador San Nicolás* and soaking in the scene is one of the many delights of a visit to Granada (photo below) → p. 66

● **Roman metropolis**
A retirement home in Andalucía was something that appealed to the Romans who built *Itálica* too. EU passport holders can wander among the ruins free of charge and marvel at the huge amphitheatre → p. 57

● **Palatial splendour**
Of all the palaces in Sevilla the *Casa de Pilatos* is special – an opulent mixture of styles from the Middle Ages, the Mudéjar and the Renaissance. And you can save the 8-euro entrance fee if you come here on a Wednesday between 3pm–7pm → p. 49

● **The different faces of Málaga**
Audio guides (available from the tourist information centre) take you on seven different tours around this coastal city free of charge → p. 81

● **3000 years of history**
The *Museo de Cádiz* takes you on a tour through the realms of ethnology, archaeology and the fine arts. A Phoenician sarcophagus and a cycle of paintings by Francisco de Zurbarán are among the highlights → p. 78

● **Mornings In the Mezquita**
Experience Córdoba's main attraction between 8.30am–10am on weekdays when a service is being held (of course without disturbing it). Let the building cast its spell on you as you listen to the Catholic mass surrounded by Islamic architecture → p. 38

◖●●●● Dots in guidebook refer to 'Best of ...' tips

● *Gripping scenes*

Watching floats weighing several tonnes being carried on people's shoulders during *Semana Santa* is moving even for those who are not religious. Sevilla (photo) is the main centre for the processions of penitents. In Úbeda the singing is particularly mournful → p. 118

● *Jumbles of white dice*

Whitwashed houses are typical of Andalucían villages. And those perched on mountain slopes are especially picturesque. But there are few white towns as pretty as *Vejer de la Frontera* → p. 83

● *Sublime beaches*

320 days of sun – the *Playa del Mónsul* and the adjoining beach, Medialuna, near San José are a dream. Crystal-clear water and fine sand in a volcanic landscape → p. 62

● *A sea of olive trees*

There are more than 60 million olive trees in the south of Spain – mostly in Jaén province. This rather monotonous landscape has a magic of its own that can best be experienced from up high. For example from the Plaza Santa Lucía in *Úbeda* → p. 75

● *DIY Flamenco*

Flamenco dancing is infectious so why not learn a few steps yourself? Go for it! Try it out at the *Flamenco Centre* in Sevilla. It's just as much fun at the *Carmen de Torres* dance studio too → p. 54

● *The Moorish legacy*

The beauty of Islamic architecture even made many a Christian conqueror go weak at the knees – such as Peter the Cruel. His residence, the *Reales Alcázares* in Sevilla, was very much on a par with the Alhambra → p. 52

● *Keeping cool*

Gazpacho, the cold soup for hot weather, has come a long way. The mixture of fresh tomatoes, peppers and dried bread was originally a dish for poorer people. Many gourmet chefs nowadays however have turned it into a supreme delicacy. For example at *El Churrasco* in Córdoba or in Málaga at *José Carlos García* → p. 40, 89

ONLY IN

BEST OF ...

● *The master of modern art*
At last you can take some time to admire the unique collection of some 200 works in the *Picasso Museum* in Málaga → **p. 88**

● *Bodegas tours*
Sherry and Andalucía – two inseparable greats. And that means of course Jerez de la Frontera and its *bodegas*. Sample one of the fascinating *guided tours* (photo) → **p. 84**

● *The art of the Iberians*
So it's off to the *Museo de Jaén*! Marvel at the warriors of old and the wolf's head finely chiselled out of stone → **p. 74**

● *Count the fish and keep dry*
At the *Acuario Almuñécar* you can watch moray eels, cuttlefish and seahorses safely from behind the armoured glass → **p. 72, 116**

● *Tornado alarm!*
Find out how much electricity you can generate on a bicycle at the *Parque de las Ciencias*, how a tornado develops and how easy it is to deceive the senses. Children and adults will have lots of fun here, playing, trying things out and marvelling at the results → **p. 117**

● *A walk on the beach*
When the clouds touch the ground and the wind is blowing a gale head for this spot not far from the Strait of Gibraltar. Walk headlong into the wind and the rain on the beach near the sleepy village of *Bolonia*. It's quite an experience → **p. 100**

● *Flamenco at its best*
An evening full of passion and emotion does wonders to help you forget the rain or buck up your spirits. Head, for example, for the *Tablao Cardenal* in Córdoba → **p. 41**

RAIN

RELAX AND CHILL OUT
Take it easy and spoil yourself

● *Arabian nights*
The walls are a dark red, the tepidarium a shimmering turquoise; Moorish horseshoe arches, domes and that Morocco feel all contribute to the good-feel factor in the hamam in Córdoba → **p. 40**

● *Peace in the city centre*
A dip in the roof-top pool does the world of good after a shopping trip or touring the sites. Spoil yourself silly in the designer spa at the *EME Fusion* hotel – and take your evening drink up on the roof too. The view of Sevilla by night is simply fantastic (photo below) → **p. 55**

● *Around Cádiz in La Pepa*
Soak up the magic of Cádiz and experience this ancient and wonderful city from the *excursion boat – La Pepa*. It leaves from the harbour several times a day, circles half of the Old Town and takes you to sandy La Caleta – to pick you up again 1½ hours later → **p. 80**

● *That VIP beach feeling*
Just lazying around on the beach all day – how boring! Relax on a daybed, cool off in the infinity pool, balance body and soul doing yoga. In the luxurious surroundings of the *Purobeach* club you will feel like a film star. Where? In Marbella, of course → **p. 16**

● *A patio with patina*
Carmona, with its churches and palaces, is a far cry from crowded Sevilla and Córdoba. The *Alcázar del Rey Don Pedro* in the 14th-century Moorish fortress is one of the most beautiful Paradors in Spain. Lose all sense of time in the Mudéjar courtyard with its fountains → **p. 56**

● *Rest awhile*
A city like Sevilla can be pretty tiring. The *Parque de María Luisa* is perfect for a siesta. The site of the Ibero-American Exposition in 1929 is now a landscaped park with lots of water features and greenery. The benches on the Plaza de España are ideal for a good read – just put your feet up and relax → **p. 51**

INTRODUCTION

DISCOVER ANDALUCÍA!

Sun and sea, bullfights and flamenco, proud people and magnificent Moorish arte-facts – this is the picture we have of Spain. And all of these are to be found in Andalucía, that part of Europe closest to Africa. For almost 800 years Arab culture shaped the face of this country and left such treasures as the Alhambra in Granada and the Mezquita in Córdoba. As a holiday destination this area of Spain offers such a variety of things and everyone is certain to find what they are looking for – sand or snow, peaceful corners or vibrant resorts, opulent luxury or the simple life of the south.

The *pueblos blancos* – the 'white towns' – with their narrow, twisty streets, secluded courtyards, lemon, orange and olive trees clambering picturesquely up ancient walls are fascinating indeed. Old fortresses perch on rugged mountain tops and magnificent churches and cathedrals testify to an Islamic and Catholic past. On top of this you will

Photo: The white mountain village, Casares, in Málaga province

An empty beach on the Costa de la Luz on the Atlantic coast

find sun, sea and beaches galore as well as virtually unlimited possibilities for sports – riding, sailing, surfing or golf, everything is available, with hiking and mountain biking, for instance, becoming increasingly popular in the forested Sierra de Aracena, the Sierra Nevada and in the Natural Park near Cazorla. And in the mountainous regions in the south it is quite possible that you will come across vultures, eagles and other wild creatures too.

What is so special and unique about the culture and way of life in Andalucía can best be explained through its history. Conquerors from North Africa made the greatest difference. After the Moors led by Tariq ibn Ziyad crossed the Strait of Gibraltar in 711 virtually all the Iberian peninsula fell into their hands in the eight years that followed. But nowhere else in Spain are traces of the Islamic culture so evident as in Andalucía

From 2500BC
Megalithic culture

1100BC
Cádiz is founded by the Phoenicians

206BC
Beginning of rule under the Romans

409AD
Visigoths spread across the Iberian peninsula

711
Tarik lands near Gibraltar and spearheads the Arabic conquest of the Iberian peninsula

8th–11th centuries
Economic and cultural heyday under Islamic rule

where much has survived over the centuries – first and foremost the Alhambra that represents the culmination in the dominance of Arabic culture in western Europe as well as its end, and the Mezquita in Córdoba, the huge mosque of a city once ruled by Caliphs. The Mudéjar style with its decorative brickwork and coloured tiles impressively displayed on the Plaza de España in Sevilla, was popular well into the 20th century. The history of some other buildings is only apparent at second glance – the Giralda, for instance, the massive cathedral bell tower in Sevilla, was originally a minaret. The region's Islamic past most probably contributed to the dominant role played by the church and religion in Spanish society and politics through the centuries.

Roman Catholicism was the only legal religion during the Franco regime with the church becoming a dubious pawn caught up in power politics. To this day its role still divides opinion. Despite the popular processions during the *Semana Santa*, the Holy Week, and the many other church holidays, Andalucía is nevertheless actually much more worldly and multicultural than you would think at first. The Islamic-Andalucían past has seen a certain resurgence recently – on the one hand, in the form of a tourist marketing strategy that has degraded the magic of the 'Arabian Nights'

> **Traces of 800 years of Arab culture**

to an inane decorative element. On the other hand, since the beginning of the 1990s, Spain has seen a massive increase in the number of immigrants from Latin America, Eastern Europe and North Africa. With the growing number of Muslims their culture and religion have become visible once again. This is not only evident in Granada in

Mid 11th–15th centuries
Formation of small Islamic principalities. Catholic armies advance as far as Andalucía that then falls to Castile – except for the Kingdom of Granada

1492
Isabella of Castile and Ferdinand of Aragón capture Granada. Expulsion of Jews and Muslims. Columbus discovers America

1516
Charles V becomes the first ruler of the Habsburg dynasty in Spain

1714
The Bourbons ascend the Spanish throne. Gibraltar becomes British

the number of tea and souvenir shops selling Moroccan crafts but also in the first new mosque in Andalucía built in the Albaicín district. In a country that defines itself through the Reconquista – the Christian conquest that lasted more than 800 years – this has inevitably led to tension. Some refuse to allow Muslims to hold their highly symbolic Friday prayer in the Mezquita in Córdoba; on the other hand there are radical tendencies to be seen that dream of a new rule in Al Andalus.

History however has not stood still anywhere, especially in the large cities such as Granada, Sevilla and Málaga. The changes in the regional capital, Sevilla, are the most obvious. A vibrant scene has emerged here which welcomes the move into a modern era, rather like that in Barcelona in the 1990s, with hip and unconventional fashion outlets, trendy bars and restaurants. The traditional Sevilla, with its fraternities, worshipping of the Virgin Mary and the *Feria de Abril* however has remained unaffected. And it is precisely the fact that these different attitudes and styles can exist at the same time which makes Andalucía such a thrilling place to be.

Clichés are still part of a lively tradition

The fascination for this southern region has a longer history that that of mass tourism which began in the 1960s. Back in the 19th century the exoticism of the flamenco and the culture of the *gitanos*, as the Romani people are known in Spain, captured people's imagination. On your trip to Andalucía you will see that many supposed clichés still form part of a lively tradition. They are part of everyday life – or, more precisely, of the annual calendar. Modern-day Spain also means that old and fascinating aspects, as well as dark and gruesome ones, are becoming increasingly rare. Bullfighting, to cite a well-known example, now prohibited in far-off Catalonia, is also the subject of controversy in this region, the birthplace of the *corrida*. How long it will survive is probably just a question of time. That cannot be said of flamenco. Beyond the *tablao* shows held in the tourist centres, this passionate art form is continuing to evolve. Arabic inspired melodies and the complicated rhythm can also be found in modern-day pop music. The 8.4 million people, living in an area the size of Portugal, have long been part of the 21st century. To gain a balanced picture of the region the picturesquely gnarled olive tree has to be seen together with the miles of monotonous plantations in the northeast of Andalucía, and Moorish palaces and the famous white towns together with the dreary,

1805
The Battle of Trafalgar

1808–14
The Peninsular War against Napoleon

1936
Franco sparks the Spanish Civil War and establishes an authoritarian regime after his victory in 1939. Beginning of dictatorship

1975
Franco dies. Juan Carlos I becomes king. Restoration of the monarchy. Transition to a democracy

1981
Andalucía becomes autonomous with its own regional government

A meeting place with tradition – the Confitería Campana in Sevilla

look-a-like blocks of flats and modern holiday homes that have now spread down more than two thirds of the coastline. The construction boom that created jobs and an economic upturn in Spain at the beginning of the 21st century has a flip side in the form of illegal building and the loss of the natural environment. New legislation now protects the coastline and positive developments can be seen in the field of nature conservancy with an increase in the use of renewable energy. Huge areas in the *Altiplanos* near La Calahorra are covered in solar panels and countless wind turbines populate the Strait of Gibraltar.

Andalucía is a picture-book of different types of scenery – dunes along the Atlantic coast, cork and holm oak forests in the northwest, mountains in the Sierra de Grazalema, semi-desert areas near Almería and olive groves around Jaén. A trip through this part of Spain is a feast for all the senses. *¡Bienvenido a Andalucía!*

1986
Spain joins the EEC (now EU)

1992
Sevilla hosts the Universal Exposition (Expo '92)

2007
A record 8.52 million tourists visit Andalucía

2008
Regional elections – the Socialist party in Andalucía wins

2008–2012
Housing slump and world economic crisis cripple Andalucía

2012
Cádiz is the Ibero-American Culture Capital

WHAT'S HOT

1 Alternative Andalucía

Tea with a difference The alternative lifestyle scene in Andalucía is concentrated in the Alpujarra region and offers everything from holistic medicine to oriental dancing and organic restaurants. The place to meet is in a *tetería*, a Moorish-style tea room *(photo)*. In *Baraka (C/Estación 12 | Órgiva)* 'Arabian Nights' are held with dancing and music. The Buddhist monastery *O sel Ling (near Órgiva)* is perfect for meditating. The restaurant *Caserío Ananda (Cortes de la Frontera)* has received several awards for its natural produce.

Flamenco fashion

2

Hot Andalucía is experiencing a new flamenco fashion fad. Brightly coloured material, embroidery and *volants* – the modern flamenco look stands out a mile and takes a bit of courage to wear. The designer Pol Núñez's interpretation of the look is very sexy *(Antonia Díaz 31 | Sevilla)*. *Charfal (Clothing Box Outlet | Los Bermejales | Avda. de Finlandia 16)* is more casual. Talented designers such as Juana Martín present their designs at the annual *International Flamenco Fashion Show (Palacio de Exposiciones y Congresos | Avda. Alcalde Luis Uruñuela 1)* in Sevilla *(photo)*.

3 Paradise on earth

... or rather on sand Nothing but the best for Marbella's beachcombers. In *La Cabane (Hotel Los Monteros | Ctra. Cádiz at km 187)* you can relax on four-posters and splash around in a designer pool. Designer sunbeds and caviar nibbles at the pool are available at ● *Purobeach (Laguna Village | Playa el Padrón | Ctra. Cádiz at km 159; photo)* and at the elegant *Ocean Club Marbella (Avda. Lola Flores)*.

Cutting-edge art scene

Surreal meets Pop Art Young artists like to model themselves on Andy Warhol and Salvador Dalí. The poster-like portraits by the painter Lara Kaló of Granada are bright and cheerful *(www.myspace.com/larakalo)*. Works by Angel Perdomo, also from Granada's art scene, have a surreal dream-like quality *(www.myspace.com/angelperdomo_arte; photo)*. These talented artists are backed by the *Estudio de Tatuajes y Piercing Pupa Tattoo Art Gallery (Granada | C/Molinos 15 | www.pupa tattooartgallery.blogspot.com)*, which regularly displays works by Lara, Angel and other newcomers. The *Montana Shop & Gallery (Sevilla | C/Arjona 9 | www.montanacolors.com)* helps make modern art media such as graffiti, installation and video art more accessible to a broader public. For cutting-edge blogging check out *Underground Art Granada (subculturagranada.wordpress.com)*.

4

Double the fun

Surfing plus Andalucía is a paradise for climbers – and also for surfers, kiters, yogis and riders. The more adventurous can combine a couple of disciplines while on holiday too. *Girasol Andalusian Tours(C/Colón 12)* offers double the fun with two-day courses in each case for kiting and climbing in Tarifa. Yoga and climbing weeks at the *Climbing Lodge (El Chorro | www.klettern-in-spanien.de – click icon for English)* complement each other perfectly. Apart from yoga *(photo)* massages help relax tired muscles. Riding can be combined with a surfing holiday at the *Hotel Dos Mares (Tarifa | Ctra. N 340 at km 79.5)*.

5

IN A NUTSHELL

ANDALUCÍAN BAROQUE

Goods unloaded off the small, heavily-laden ships that arrived in the port of Sevilla from Spain's new colonies heralded in the country's 'Golden Age' – literally. The 'Siglo de Oro' ensured that artists' order books were kept full in the 17th century. Francisco Pacheco (1564–1654) is considered the founder of the Seville School of Painting. His pupils included Diego Velázquez (1599–1660), the great master of Spanish Baroque painting. Bartolomé Murillo (1618–82) and the 'painter of monks' Francisco de Zurbarán (1598–1664) also worked in Sevilla.

At that time, an equally realistic and striking style evolved in the south of Spain in the field of sculpture too. Master sculptors include Pedro de Mena, Juan de Mesa, Pedro Roldán and Martínez de Montañés.

ANDASOL

Little rain and lots of sun – perfect not just for holiday-makers. On the high lying plains near La Calahorra, where the opening scene of the film *Once Upon a Time in the West* was made, things are changing. The desert landscape is no longer just an eldorado for the heroes of the Wild West. Thanks to a new energy

Flamenco, bullfighting, Picasso & Co –
a brief look at some key points in Andalucía's
social, cultural and political history

policy, the sun is now being used to generate electricity over an area the size of 210 football fields – a perfect location for the first parabolic trough power plant in Europe. Andasol 1 started operation in 2009; in the meantime Andasol 3 has also been completed. Now the largest solar power plant in the world, it generates 600 gigawatt-hours a year, enough to supply at least half a million households. Other than photovoltaic plants, the solar thermal power plant can also produce electricity at night. It does however need a lot of water.

Scientists have been carrying out solar thermal experiments in the Tabernas Desert since the 1980s and experts believe that, by 2030, Spain could meet a quarter of its electricity requirements using solar energy.

Bullfighters waiting concentratedly for their big moment

tingness and its fighting nature make it an attractive victim. The matador and his helpers, the *cuadrilla,* bait the animal with their yellow and pink *capas*. Bulls are however colourblind and are aggravated simply by the movement. Tired by its fruitless attacks, the bull has to face its next test. The *picador* enters on horseback, lance in hand, which he jabs into the bull's back. The horse is protected from the bull's horns by a padded covering and the *picador*'s right leg by a metal plate. Two of the *cuadrilla* then stick six *banderillas*, brightly coloured wooden sticks with barbs which cause pain to the bull with every movement for the rest of the fight, into the back of the animal's neck. The final act then begins. The matador (from *matar*, to kill) faces the bull alone, armed with a sword and the *muleta,* the red cloth. The art of a matador is to let the bull's lethal horns pass as closely as possible to his body and to cut a good figure. In the end, he stands in front of the bull for the final thrust. In the 'best' case, the animal stands there for a moment and then collapses.

Spanish opponents to the *corrida* find it incredibly irritating that foreigners automatically associate Spain with bullfighting. It was banned in Catalonia in 2010 and from 2012 onwards no *corridas* have been held in other autonomous regions either — something seen as an anti-Spanish success story by independence-minded Catalonia. At present, Andalucía is still a long way from such a step. This will only happen when less and less people show an interest in this bloody spectacle and it simply becomes economically unviable.

BULLFIGHTING

The *corrida* starts late in the afternoon. During the course of the evening three matadors each face two bulls in a fight that ends with a sword being thrust between the animals' shoulder blades. A *corrida* is not a fight as such but a ritualised killing. After a life on the plains the bull *(toro)* is led into the arena totally unprepared for what is to come. Its unwit-

COLUMBUS

In the 15th century only a madman could really have had the idea of setting out to sea from Europe, heading west, to find a passage to the east, to India. Christopher Columbus, called Cristóbal Colón by the Spanish, was born around 1451 in Genoa, Italy. He was convinced the world was round and tried at first to win over the Portuguese royal house to support his plan. But that fell on deaf ears. The Spanish queen Isabella, however, gave in to the cartographer and seafarer's powers of persuasion and had Columbus prepare three ships for the journey. The adventurer set off from the little Andalucían town of Palos de la Frontera on 3 August, 1492, and first sighted land again on 12 October. Unbeknown to him, Columbus had discovered America. And this marked the beginning of Spain's emergence as a world power in the 16th century.

FLAMENCO

A long drawn-out 'aaayyy' launches the lament for an unfaithful lover or a dead brother. It is not the beauty of the voice that captivates the audience but its expressive power, the depth of its emotion (jondura). The singer, either male or female, sits bolt upright on a chair, as if in a trance, egged on by the admiring calls of ¡olé! from the onlookers. The handclaps (palmas) support the complicated rhythm of the singing. There are some 40 different flamenco styles, from the melancholic siguiriya to the popular fandango. The flamenco has its beginnings in the second half of the 18th century in Cádiz, Jerez de la Frontera and the Triana district of Sevilla. The flamenco, which

Replicas of Columbus's ships near La Rábida on the banks of the Río Tinto

from the artist to the audience. Further information under *www.andalucia.org/flamenco*

MIGRATION

In the 1960s and early '70s hundreds of thousands of Andalucíans moved away in search of a better life in the north of Spain, Switzerland, Germany and France. And since the 1980s the wave of emigration has turned into immigration The British and Germans have settled along the beautful shores of this region whereas the towns have attracted Romanians, Moroccans, Ecuadorians and others from Latin America. Every now and again, boats packed with illegal immigrants, *pateras*, land on the Andalucían coast. Young, well qualified Spaniards in particular have been leaving their native country during the current economic crisis in the hope of finding a job elsewhere.

PICASSO

Pablo Ruiz Picasso (1881–1973), the 20th-century artist and genius, came from Málaga, but only spent a few years of his childhood there. When his father, an art teacher, was offered a job in La Coruña, the family moved to far-off Galicia in 1891 and not long afterwards to Barcelona. After the Spanish Civil War Picasso never wanted to set foot in his native country again as long as it was still under the rule of the dictator, Franco. And nothing ever became of the artist's dream of showing his work in the city he was born in either. In 1953, Picasso sent two lorry loads of paintings to Málaga, intended to be shown in the Palacio de Buenavista. However, this was prohibited by the Franco regime. 50 years later, that very palacio has been turned into the centrepiece of the new Picasso Museum which houses 155 works given by Christine Ruiz-Picasso, the widow of Picasso's first son Paolo.

Affordable as a postcard – a 'Picasso'

has its roots in Sinti and Roma music and Andalucían folk music, reached its heyday in 1860–1910. Even then, the dance performed to the music proved to be a huge attraction to a wide public. The accompanying guitar music also established itself. Most *flamencos* are Roma and are convinced that a *payo* (non-Roma) would never be able to achieve the same depth of artistic expression. The flamenco performed on the stages in tourist *tablaos* is generally of the more cheerful variety with the dancing taking pride of place. That does not mean that the quality of the performance is lower than elsewhere. But you will seldom come across the *duende* (goblin), the secret flamenco magician who transports the sparks of emotion

PUEBLOS BLANCOS

Virtually all villages in the south of Spain are white. But, in addition to its whitewashed houses a *pueblo blanco* needs to have narrow streets in which you can easily get lost to become a real tourist attraction. And only then can you assume that the village was originally a Moorish settlement. On top of that, it should be perched picturesquely on the side of a mountain or a rocky outcrop. Whitewashing houses first became popular in the 17th century and was traditionally part of a woman's work in the home. Vejer and Arcos de la Frontera, Grazalema, Gaucín, Casares and Frigiliana are especially pretty *pueblos blancos*.

ROMANI PEOPLE

The number of *gitanos* (gypsies) in the country is open to speculation. The most reliable estimates are of 650,000–700,000 – around 2% of the population of Spain. Some 300,000 live in Andalucía where the first *gitanos* settled in the 15th century. They have however remained a people within a people. Their aim is not integration but to maintain their cultural independence. *Gitanos* and *payos* (non-Roma) live side by side without understanding each other's way of life. According to surveys the Spanish do not disapprove of any other minority as much as the Roma, even though they have enriched Spanish culture with the flamenco. Infant mortality among the Romani people is still high, their life expectancy low and their time at school short. The foundation *Fundación Segretariado Gitano* aims to improve 'professional qualification and social participation without impairing the traditions of the gypsy culture'. A challenge for the whole of society.

SEMANA SANTA

Swaying *pasos* (platforms) on which figures of the Passion of Christ or the Virgin Mary are carried through the streets surrounded by a sea of candles, mournful processions, bare-footed penitents with pointed hoods that come down over the faces. This is the picture we have of 'Holy Week'in Andalucía and this is how it really is – especially in the capital Sevilla where more than 50 fraternities *(cofradías* and *hermandades)* hold their processions. The *pasos*, sometimes weighing tonnes, are carried by *costaleros*. When the Black Death was running rife in Málaga strong, healthy men were rare and help was sought form the town jail. This tradition has been maintained to this day and, every year, one prisoner in Malaga willing to act as a bearer can hope to be pardoned.

TORO DE OSBORNE

Drivers can see the silhouette of a bull from a long way down the road. The 12m (40ft)-high figure has been advertising for the sherry and brandy manufacturer, Osborne, from El Puerto de Santa María, since 1957. But the animal has long since become more than that, namely a symbol of Spain itself. When a law was passed in 1989 prohibiting advertising on country roads, Osborne removed the writing but not the animal – for which the company was given a fine in 1994. After protests from thousands of Spaniards parliament declared that the animal was part of the country's cultural heritage and was therefore allowed to be left there. An almost bigger surprise is the silhouette of a donkey on the A4 between Bailén and Córdoba that dominates the landscape. The 'Burro de Cataluña' was invented by two young Catalans in 2004. It was an ironic response to the popular Osborne bull and first cropped up as a car sticker. It has now become a symbol of Catalan's struggle for independence.

FOOD & DRINK

Well, if that doesn't wake you up! The new day in Andalucía is welcomed in with a cup of blacker-than-black coffee that even with lots of hot milk turns merely a dark brown. And this is often only accompanied by *a bollo*, a sweet bun. Breakfast must have been invented in another corner of the world.

Spanish coffee, prepared rather like an Italian *espresso*, is praised by aficionados – but that might not be much consolation. However, a more typical breakfast includes a *tostada*, toasted white bread eaten with butter and jam, olive oil and salt or oil, salt and tomato purée. The Spanish equivalent of a French croissant is called a *cruasán*

and is rarely available without icing. And as it's really sticky, you eat it with a knife and fork.

At around 11am the Andalucíans leave their offices for a second breakfast. It may be rather like the first in principle but some people order a small glass of beer and a *tapa*, a little savoury snack. In many Andalucían bars, that are generally a cross between a bar and a cafeteria, a tapa is served with a softdrink or alcohol. If you want to order more, simply point to whatever takes your fancy in the glass display cabinet and ask for *una tapa de esto* – 'one of these'. What bars and restaurants offer as tapas (*tapa* is a descrip-

---

Photo: The terrace at the Hotel Alhambra Palace in Granada

A tapas bar, gourmet temple or a pub? Wherever you decide to go, you can expect a culinary treat

tion of quantity not a type of food) can also be ordered as a *ración* (portion) for several people. If you are alone, half a portion *(media ración)* is enough to fill you up. If you're hungry from swimming, head for the next *chiringuito*, a beach snackbar with tapas and *raciónes*, providing one still exists – the Spanish coastal preservation law no longer allows buildings on beaches.

Lunch is eaten between 2pm and 4.30pm. Restaurants all over Andalucía have lunch menus *(menú del día)* from 8 euros upwards. You normally have a choice of three starters *(primero)* and three main courses *(segundo);* a pudding and a glass of table wine are included in the price. The more locals at the tables, the better the place is likely to be. The Andalucían cuisine is as varied as the region itself. Fish and

LOCAL SPECIALITIES

▶ **ajoblanco** – cold garlic soup with crushed almonds and grapes
▶ **albóndigas** – meatballs
▶ **bacalao** – salted and dried cod
▶ **boquerones fritos/en vinagre** – anchovies, fried or in vinegar
▶ **café solo/cortado/con leche** – espresso/espresso with a little milk/ white coffee
▶ **chorizo** – salami with red peppers
▶ **churros** – fried doughnuts (popular at breakfast *con chocolate*)
▶ **clara** – beer with *gaseosa* (like shandy)
▶ **ensaladilla rusa** – Spanish potato salad
▶ **gambas al ajillo** – prawns in garlic sauce
▶ **gaseosa** – lemonade
▶ **gazpacho** – cold vegetable soup made with tomato purée, cucumber, peppers, oil and vinegar (photo above left)

▶ **horchata** – refreshing, bitter drink made of tigernuts
▶ **jamón** – dry cured serrano ham, the best comes from Jabugo in the Sierra de Aracena and Trevélez in the Alpujarras
▶ **mejillones** – mussels
▶ **pescaítos** – mixed platter of fried fish and seafood depending on the season
▶ **pimientos** – peppers
▶ **pulpo/calamares/chipirones** – octopus/calamares/squid
▶ **queso** – cheese, generally *manchego* – from La Mancha (as as a tapa or for breakfast)
▶ **salmorejo** – similar to gazpacho, but thicker, with puréed bread (as a tapa with bread)
▶ **tortilla** – Spanish omelette, generally with slices of pototo. As a tapa order *un pincho de tortilla,* a slice of tortilla (photo above right)

seafood can be found everywhere close to the sea. *Gambas* and *langostinos* from Sanlúcar de Barrameda, as well as tuna *(atún)* are well known throughout Spain. The fact that the traditional way of cooking is relatively simple does not have a negative effect on its quality. Tomatoes, peppers and garlic are almost always present. Main courses are normally served without side dishes. A little bit of salad, a few chips and that's it. The dishes gain their special flavour from the use of olive oil, the only oil that Spaniards ever cook with. Olive oil is the basis of the 'Mediterranean diet' that nutritionists consider the secret to Spaniards' longevity.

Andalucíans do not sit down to supper until 9pm at the earliest, in summer generally much later. In Sevilla at weekends you could well go to a restaurant at 10pm and be the only guests for an hour before the place suddenly fills up.

Apart from simple, down-to-earth dishes, there is a world of refined delicacies too. Famous chefs such as Juan Mari Arzak, Martín Berasategui and the Catalan Ferran Adrià have revolutionised the art of haute cuisine *(alta cocina)* in Spain. A younger generation of dedicated chefs is following in their footsteps in Andalucía too. They 'deconstruct' and whisk things into aromatic froths, conjure up hot and cold layered creations and turn regional and exotic recipes into new delights to tickle the palate.

Cooking has become a mixture of science and art. Favourites at the moment include Dani García *(Restaurant Calima | Hotel Don Pepe | C/José Meliá | Marbella | tel. 952 764 252)* and Benito Gómez *(Tragabuches | C/José Aparicio 1 | Ronda | tel. 952 190 291)*.

The ultimate *jamón ibérico* comes from the northwest of Andalucía. Gourmets consider it the best ham in the world. Keep an eye out for the additional wording *de bellota*. This means that it is from free-range Ibérico pigs that have gorged themselves on acorns.

Andalucía's most famous alcoholic beverage is the *vino de Jerez* – called sherry everywhere else in the world. It is a potent, fortified wine grown on chalky soil in the sherry triangle between Jerez de la Frontera, Puerto de Santa María and Sanlúcar de Barrameda. The barrels of sherry are stored in *bodegas* above ground in rows three or four barrels high. The youngest sherry at the top, the oldest at the bottom. The sherry to be sold is taken

from the bottom row. The barrels are then filled with the wine from the row above that blends with the older wine below. This process is repeated until the barrels at the top need to be filled with new wine.

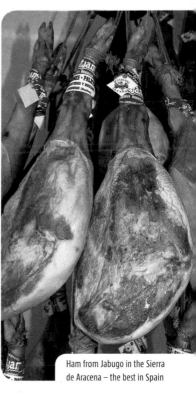

Ham from Jabugo in the Sierra de Aracena – the best in Spain

This method ensures that the taste remains the same. Vintage sherry therefore does not exist. The most famous styles of sherry are the dry *fino* and *manzanilla* from Sanlúcar de Barrameda. Both should be drunk chilled. *Amontillado*, *cream* and *oloroso* sherries are more mild. *Pedro ximénez* is sweet and heavy. Excellent brandy is also matured in sherry barrels – here the maxim 'the older the better' holds true.

SHOPPING

Whoever wants something from Andalucía to take back home will find any amount of hand-crafted souvenirs. Ceramics are particularly popular. Shops are allowed to be open for 12 hours a day from Monday to Saturday, and on eight Sundays a year. The siesta is sacred to Spaniards and most shops are open from 10am–1.30pm and only open again in the evening from 5pm–8.30pm.

CERAMICS

Simple shapes with elaborate patterns prevail, mostly with plant-like motifs painted in bold brushstrokes in blues, yellows and greens. At first glance these may seem a little rustic and kitschy, but there's no escaping their charm. Perhaps not so pretty but very practical are *cuencos* – dishes and bowls. *Azulejos*, tiles with geometrical or plant patterns generally inspired by the Moorish tradition, are also extremely popular. If you find something you like, don't hesitate – buy it! It won't necessarily be cheaper anywhere else and the shop might not be open when you return.

FOOD

Andalucían specialities to be drunk or eaten are also popular souvenirs. As with wine, good olive oil depends on where it comes from. Go for the 'extra native olive oil' *(aceite de oliva virgen extra)*. The fact that olive oil from different D.O.s *(denominación de orígen)* varies in smell, colour and taste is generally due to the different olives harvested (there are more than 200 varieties). Assistants in specialist shops such as the *Casa de Aceite,* located in Baeza and Úbeda, will be happy to advise you.

The best ham in Spain is called *jamón ibérico de bellota* and comes from Jabugo. The dry-cured haunches come from a breed of pig that is only found in Spain and is traditionally fed on acorns. The best serrano ham comes from Trevélez where it is dried in the cool mountain air of the Alpujarras.

HANDICRAFTS

Leather goods artistically decorated with silver paint are a speciality of Córdoba

Shopping in Andalucía is fun – whether for hand-crafted items, affordable fashions or the latest trends

in particular. Granada is famous for its marquetry. There is a huge selection of items from boxes of all sizes to chessboards. Less exclusive but very practical are blankets from Grazalema and unusual *jarapas* (rugs) from Frigiliana or the Alpujarras.

SHERRY

Andalucía's most famous wine is sherry from Jerez, El Puerto de Santa Maria or Sanlúcar de Barrameda. Take a guided tour of a *bodega* and sample the different varieties. *Fino* and *manzanilla* are dry and refreshing. The latter is only made in Sanlúcar de Barrameda. The amber coloured *amontillado* is also dry; its spicy nutty aroma is the perfect accompaniment to tapas with cheese and meat. The dark, sweet *oloroso* and *pedro ximénez* are the perfect match for desserts.

SHOES & CLOTHES

Good leather articles can be found in Ubrique (Sierra de Grazalema), the best riding boots in Valverde del Camino (Provinz Huelva). Shoes and clothes in Andalucía are generally a good buy. Take a look in the popular fashion outlets Zara, Mango and Hoss in larger towns. If you are after the latest trends, go to Sevilla. This is not only the home of Andalucía's most famous fashion designer, *Victorio & Lucchino (Calle Sierpes)*, but also of many small but exquisite boutiques.

SILVER

If you fancy something more upmarket take a look at the silverwork in Córdoba in particular. A proper jeweller *(joyería)* is your best bet for genuine, high-quality items.

THE PERFECT ROUTE

FANTASTIC PLACES TO SWIM

Start off from ❶ *Málaga* → p. 87. Driving along the A7 heading east you will generally keep the sea in view. Take a stroll around ❷ *Nerja* → p. 94 to the Balcón de Europa, a terrace with wonderful views. There are fantastic bays below you, just perfect for a swim. In ❸ *Salobreña* → p. 73 a little further on, climb up through the steep Old Town (photo left). Or perhaps you'd rather head for the local beach to cool off.

THE BEAUTY OF THE ALHAMBRA

Leave the coast at Motril and head inland through the Alpujarras and the Sierra Nevada to ❹ *Granada* → p. 64. Spend the afternoon in the centre and the Albaicín district before watching a flamenco show in one of the caves in Sacromonte. Devote the next morning entirely to the Alhambra whose beauty will keep your mind spinning as you head off through the Sierra Subbética to Córdoba.

MOORISH HISTORY

After visiting the Mezquita and the Old Town of ❺ *Córdoba* → p. 36 you won't be able to get enough art and culture. So head off to the ruins of the former Caliphate town ❻ *Madinat al-Zahra* → p. 42 and discover more about Arabian-Christian history.

LIFE ON THE GUADALQUIVIR

Stay at least one day and one night in ❼ *Sevilla* → p. 48 – long enough to see the highlights. The cathedral, the Reales Alcázares and the unique atmosphere of the city on the Guadalquivir are sure to stay with you for some time (photo right).

THE LAND OF SHERRY

Now head for ❽ *Jerez de la Frontera* → p. 83 through lovely countryside with a light-coloured *albariza* chalky soil in which the sherry grape is grown. It's a good idea to book a tour of a *bodega* in advance before setting off around the town. Finish off the day with some tapas in the centre.

THE STORMY COSTA DE LA LUZ

Our route continues to Sanlúcar de Barrameda. Well rested, carry on to the oldest city on the Peninsula – in fact, in the whole of Europe – ❾ *Cádiz* → p. 76. The light in the 'little silver cup' as the city with its prominent

towers is called, its liberal feel (Spain's first democratic constitution was signed here in 1812) and its vibrant Old Town cast their magic spell on all visitors. After passing through Conil, picturesque ⑩ *Vejer de la Frontera → p. 83*, Barbate and Zahara de los Atunes, head along the eastern stretch of the Costa de la Luz and visit the Montenmedio art centre. Things will get a little windier when you reach ⑪ *Tarifa → p. 99*, a hotspot for surfers and the most southerly point in Europe.

THE WHITE TOWNS

After a detour to or even a stay in the former fortress ⑫ *Castellar de la Frontera → p. 100* visit some of the picturesque white villages and small towns such as ⑬ *Gaucín → p. 98*. On the approach to ⑭ *Ronda → p. 96* you will understand why writers such as Ernest Hemingway were so enthusiastic about the place. Its location on two cliff tops, the views and the picturesque collection of buildings that make up the town are second to none.

GLAMOUROUS COASTLINE

The twisty and beautiful mountain road A 376 winds its way down to the coast. After a short stop in elegant ⑮ *Puerto Banús → p. 92* carry on to ⑯ *Marbella → p. 92*, whose Old Town full of flowers will surprise you. From here it's not far to *Málaga → p. 87*. After a total of 1000km (620mi) and a head full of impressions, the port and its museum and shops will make a pleasant break.

1000km (620mi). Driving time only: 17 hours. Recommended duration of trip: 5–8 days. A detailed map of the route can be found on the back cover, in the road atlas and on the pull-out map

THE WEST

The Guadalquivir, Andalucía's lifeline, flows westwards – through Córdoba, the old caliphate city, and Sevilla, Andalucía's pulsating heart, until the river meets the Atlantic near Doñana National Park.

Córdoba's big attraction is the more than 1000-year-old Mezquita – the mosque-cathedral. Sevilla, the capital of Andalucía, is a city to be experienced. After you have soaked in the magic of the Reales Alcázares and the cathedral, immerse yourself in the city's nightlife. In the neighbouring province of Huelva, the long beaches on the western Costa de la Luz, the Doñana and the little-visited Sierra de Aracena are all inviting destinations.

ARACENA

(137 D2) *(∅ C3)* **The scent of the forests and their greenery, like a refreshing shower of rain at the end of a hot summer's day, can be enjoyed on walks between one half-forgotten village and the next through meadows shaded by chestnut and olive trees, cork and holm oaks.**

Sevillians have long since discovered the forested hills in the Natural Park ★ *Sierra de Aracena y Picos de Aroche (www.sierra dearacena.com)*, at the western end of the Sierra Morena, to escape the seering

---

Photo: The Plaza de España in Sevilla

Lively cities and lovely countryside – explore the many sites in Sevilla and Córdoba and soak up the pure zest for life

heat of the city for a few days of relaxation. Now others are starting to explore this lovely stretch of countryside in a forgotten corner of Andalucía. The little town of *Aracena* with a population of 8000 is the geographical and tourist centre of the park. The hill town is a particularly inviting spot to spend a few quiet days, enjoying evenings in the bars on the Gran Vía and Plaza Marqués de Aracena. The casino on

this square from 1910 in the Andalucían Art Deco style is eye-catching. The Plaza Alta, originally enclosed by the walls of the Old Town, is an inviting place for a stroll. The town hall is also noteworthy. Together with the mighty *Parroquía de la Asunción* that has just recently been restored, these two buildings are among the most beautiful examples of local Renaissance architecture. The *Museo del Jamón* – the ham

The view from above Aracena

museum – *(Gran Vía)* on the green Plaza Doña Elvira is devoted solely to the Black Iberian pig. The ruins of a Portuguese castle, cheek by jowl with the Gothic church *Nuestra Señora del Mayor Dolor*, is perched on the 🔆 top of the hill above the town, watching over the goings-on down below.

SIGHTSEEING

GRUTA DE LAS MARAVILLAS
The 'Grotto of Marvels' is a cave with stalactites and stalagmites, accessible over a length of 1200m. *Daily 10am–1.30pm and 3pm–6pm | admission 8.50 euros | C/Pozo de la Nieve | bookings tel. 6 63 93 78 76*

FOOD & DRINK

JOSÉ VICENTE
The best restaurant in town with its own delicatessen. *Closed Tue (reservations essential in the evening) | Avda. Andalucía 53 | tel. 9 59 12 84 55 | Moderate–Expensive*

MONTECRUZ
Delicious tapas and tasty local dishes; game specialities served during the hunting season (Oct–Dec). *Closed Wed | Plaza San Pedro | tel. 9 59 12 60 13 | Budget–Moderate*

WHERE TO STAY

FINCA VALBONO
3-star hotel in a delightful, beautifully restored *cortijo* (country house) just outside Aracena. *30 rooms and apartments | Ctra. Carboneras, 1km (about ½mi) | tel. 9 59 12 77 11 | www.fincavalbono.com | Moderate*

INSIDER TIP ▶ HOTEL LA ERA DE ARACENA 🔆
Stylish country hotel in a lovely location with the best views of the *sierra*. Perfect for a romantic weekend. *16 rooms | N 433, 85.4km (53mi) | tel. 9 6 10 79 68 00 | www.hotelaracena.com | Budget–Moderate*

HOTEL LOS CASTAÑOS
Time seems to have stood still here. This typical town hotel is a comfortable place to stay. *30 rooms and apartments | Avda. Huelva 5 | tel. 9 59 12 63 00 | www.los castanoshotel.com | Budget*

INFORMATION

Oficina de Turismo (tel. 6 63 93 78 77) at the entrance to the Gruta de las Maravillas. Information on the Natural Park from the *Centro de Interpretación del Parque Natural (Plaza Alta | half way to the castle). www. aracena.es*

WHERE TO GO

INSIDER TIP **ALMONASTER LA REAL**
(136 C2) (*ฒ B3*)
The most picturesque village in the Sierra (pop. 1800, 27km/17mi west of Aracena). The fortress and mosque from the 10th century, perched on a hilltop, were built on the foundations of a Visigothic basilica. The ☆ minaret offers a view second to none, taking in the bullfighting arena (19th century) that is located next to the fortress and clings to the hillside like a much too big swallows' nest. Accommodation can be found in the *Hotel Casa García (22 rooms | C/San Martín 2 | tel. 9 59 14 31 09 | Budget)* with its own restaurant. Jabugo, famous throughout Spain for its ham, is not far away. In the last few months of their lives the pigs are fed nothing but acorns from holm oaks.

FUENTEHERIDOS AND ALÁJAR
(136 C2) (*ฒ C3*)
The village *Fuenteheridos* (pop. 700), 11km (7mi) west of Aracena, is surrounded by chestnut and holm oak forests. Its narrow lanes have made many a driver despair. A fountain with twelve taps on the central square *El Coso* recalls the wealth of water found on this spot. Andalucían cooking is available at the rustic *Restaurante Biarritz (C/Charneca 13 | tel. 9 59 12 50 88 | Budget)*. Not far away is the family-run *Hostal Carballo (7 rooms | C/La Fuente 16 | tel. 9 59 12 51 08 | www.hostalcarballo.com | Budget)*.

★ **Sierra de Aracena**
Forested, rugged, mountainous area with vultures, eagles and wolves. Perfect for outdoor types → **p. 32**

★ **Mezquita**
This magical Moorish forest of stone columns is Córdoba's most famous landmark → **p. 38**

★ **Barrio Santa Cruz**
Sevilla'a fairy tale-like former Jewish Quarter → **p. 49**

★ **Catedral and Giralda**
Sevilla – a Catholic cathedral watched over by a old minaret → **p. 50**

★ **Madinat al-Zahra**
Wander around this beautiful palace-city where the Caliphs of Córdoba once lived in extravagant luxury → **p. 42**

★ **Reales Alcázares**
A Christian king had a Moorish jewel and delightful gardens created in the heart of Sevilla → **p. 52**

★ **Parque Nacional Coto de Doñana**
This national park in the Guadalquivir estuary is Europe's largest bird sanctuary → **p. 45**

MARCO POLO HIGHLIGHTS

Alájar (pop. 800, 5km/3mi south of Fuenteheridos) is an inviting place for a cup of coffee in the shadow of *San Marcos*. This is where you will also find the organically-run country hotel and restaurant ☺ *Posada Alajar (8 rooms | C/Médico E. González 2 | tel. 9 59 12 57 12 | www. laposadadealajar.com | Budget)*.

INSIDER TIP LINARES DE LA SIERRA
(136 C2) *(ⓜ C3)*

A well-signed hiking trail leads from Aracena to Linares (pop. 300) 6km (3¾mi) away. This picturesque village still has two communal places where the locals wash their clothes *(lavaderos)* and a square which is turned into a bullfighting arena during the *Fiesta de San Juan* in June.

ZUFRE (137 D2) *(ⓜ C3)*

This little place with a population of 1000, 27km (16¾mi) east of Aracena, is reminiscent of the white towns around Ronda. The *Plaza de la Iglesia*, with the church of the *Purísima Concepción*, the Renaissance town hall and an intriguing gargoyle waterspout (16th century), is the most beautiful square.

CÓRDOBA

🔲 MAP INSIDE BACK COVER
(139 E4) *(ⓜ G3)* **The beautiful city of Córdoba (pop. 330,000) is deservedly an extremely popular tourist destination. Visitors from all over the world jostle for space in the narrow streets in the Judería area around the Mezquita. But just a few yards from the 1000-year-old mosque-cathedral the pace of life is perfectly normal.**

Take a seat in one of the bars on the Plaza Trinidad at the foot of the church of the same name and watch the locals chatting to one another at the top of their voices.

🏙 WHERE TO START?
Ronda Isasa: To explore Córdoba, visit the Mezquita or stroll around the narrow streets of the Judería district, park at the Ronda Isasa on the Guadalquivir or in the multi-storey car park at Paseo de la Victória. From the station take bus no. 3, for example, to Glorieta de Media Luna and walk from there into the Old Town.

Then go off and explore the countless little streets in the city centre which never seem to lead to where you think they should – but you will be rewarded with lots of surprising discoveries.

The Mezquita alone makes a visit to this city worthwhile. It is the legacy of the Arabs who caused Córdoba to blossom into one of the most important cities of its time at the turn of the first millennium. Córdoba would like to have been named European Capital of Culture for 2016. Despite not winning the nomination many corners of the city have recently been renovated and a contemporary art centre opened in 2013. The *Espacio Andaluz de Creación Contemporánea* (C4 for short) is on the other side of the river.

SIGHTSEEING

ALCÁZAR DE LOS REYES CRISTIANOS

Alfonso XI had the palace of the Christian kings built in the 14th century after Ferdinand III of Castile put an end to 500 years of Arabian rule in Córdoba in 1236. The *Baños Reales* (royal baths), influenced by Moorish architecture *(admission 2.25 euros)*, are unusual for a Catholic palace of that period. The *Torre de la Inquisición* is a reminder of the palace's dark past when it was used as the seat of

Façades covered with flowers are typical of Córdoba

the Inquisition in Córdoba from 1482 until 1821. Sights include finds from Roman times such as mosaics and a sarcophagus. The beautifully laid out garden is a lovely place to stroll and relax in after a tour of the Alcázar. *July–Aug Tue–Sat 8.30am–2.30pm only, otherwise in summer also 5.30pm–8.30pm, winter Tue–Sat 8.30am–7.30pm, Sun all year round 9.30am–2.30pm | admission 4.50 euros, Tue–Fri 8.30am–10.30am admission free | son et lumière March–Sept from 9pm, admission 6.80 euros*

INSIDER TIP CAPILLA MUDÉJAR

This little chapel with its wonderful Mudéjar ornamentation is now open to the public at long last. The chapel of rest from the early 15th century is richly decorated with *azulejos* and plasterwork. Inscriptions in Cufic, an early form of the Arabic alphabet, come as a surprise. *10.30am–1.30pm, 5.30pm–8.30pm, in winter 10.30am–1.30pm, 3.30pm–6.30pm, closed Sun afternoons and Mon mornings | admission free | Plaza Maimónides*

CASA DE SEFARAD

The life of Sephardi Jews (who lived on the Iberian Peninsula until their expulsion in 1492) is brought to life in this historical building in the Judería district. Interesting exhibits and a beautiful library; concerts occasionally held here. *Mon–Sat 11am–6pm, Sun 11am–2pm | admission 4 euros | www.casadesefarad.com*

JUDERÍA

At the time of the caliphates in the middle of the 10th century, many Jews moved to Córdoba and settled in the streets around the Mezquita. The period of religious tolerance ended in the 14th century under Christian rule. In 1391 the worst pogrom took place when Jews who had remained here were finally driven out in 1492 on the orders of the Catholic king. Today, the former Jewish Quarter is a Unesco World Heritage Site and swarming with tourists. Narrow streets, whitewashed buildings and courtyards full of the scent of flowers are a delight. No visit to Córdoba is complete without a walk along the *Calleja de*

The interior of the Mezquita is both magnificent and impressive

las Flores – 'Flower Lane'. Andalucía's only synagogue still in existence, built during the reign of Alfonso XI in 1315 in the Mudéjar style, is well worth a visit. *Calle Judíos 20 | Tue–Sat 9.30am–2pm, 3.30pm–5.30pm, Sun 9.30am–5pm | free admission for EU citizens*

MEZQUITA ★ ●

Entering the mosque-cathedral through the Puerta de las Palmas you find yourself in a magical forest of stone columns with long rows of red-and-white double arches, one above the other. The virtually square Mezquita at first looks as if it were perfectly symmetrical. But every step you take reveals more of the building's complex structure. The Moorish rulers of Córdoba began erecting their mosque in 785 on the site of a basilica that they had bought from the Christians. The Mezquita did not reach the dimensions it has today until around the turn of the first millennium after three major extensions. If you walk anti-clockwise around the building you will be able to trace its construction in chronological order. The columns in the first quarter of the building after the entrance are from Roman and Visigothic structures; the arches above them are made of yellowy-white sandstone and red brick. On the south-eastern side, opposite the entrance, is the *mihrab*, the magnificent prayer niche, that was added during the second major extension in the mid 10th century. The last building phase, when the Mezquita was extended to the north-east, is the least inspiring. The arches over the columns here are only painted.

After capturing Córdoba in 1236 the Christians used the Mezquita as a church, having taken a fancy to the fairy tale-like house of prayer. Over the next 300 years they were content with simply adding

2.30pm–8.30pm, Wed–Sat 9am–8.30pm, Sun 9am–2.30pm | free admission for EU citizens | Plaza de Jerónimo Páez 7

MUSEO DE BELLAS ARTES

The museum was founded in 1862 by the father of the painter Julio Romero de Torres. It houses works by major Spanish artists including Murillo, Ribera, Zurbarán and Goya. *Tue 2.30pm–8.30pm, Wed–Sat 9am–8.30pm, Sun 9am–2.30pm | free admission for EU citizens | Plaza del Potro*

PALACIO DE LOS MARQUESES DE VIANA

Córdoba's most magnificent palace dates from the 14th century and was continuously extended. Today it comprises 12 courtyards and a garden. *June–Sept Tue–Fri 10am–7pm, Sat–Sun 10am–3pm | admission 8 euros, courtyards only 5 euros | Plaza Don Gome 2*

PLAZA DE LOS DOLORES

A stone statue of Christ *(Cristo de los Faroles)* is to be found on this small 'Square of Sorrows' with oddly shaped wrought iron lanterns.

PLAZA DEL POTRO

An inviting spot like a village square in the middle of the city, dominated by the façade of the *Museo de Bellas Artes* in the Spanish, late Gothic, Plateresque style. The statue of a colt with its front legs raised above the Renaissance fountain in the middle of the square is one of Córdoba's emblems. Cervantes once spent the night in the *Posada del Potro* (15th century) overlooking the square that he immortalised in *Don Quixote*.

TORRE DE LA CALAHORRA ☼

The popular 'Museum of Three Cultures' housed in a former defensive tower (1369) takes a romanticised rather than really

small chapels that hardly effected the overall impression of the former mosque. However, in the 16th century, the bishop Alonso Manrique insisted on a cathedral being built. Despite fierce opposition from the local populace, a Renaissance church was planted in the middle of the Mezquita. To this day, nobody has dared remove the result of this act of architectural sacrilege. *March–Oct Mon–Sat 10am–7pm, Sun 8.30am–10am, 2pm–7pm, Nov–Feb Mon–Sat 10am–5pm, Sun 8.30am–10am, 2pm–5pm | admission 8 euros | services Mon–Sat 8.30am, Sun 11am*

MUSEO ARQUEOLÓGICO

Córdoba's fascinating archaeological museum boasts Neolithic ceramics, limestone sculptures from the Iberian period (6th–3rd centuries BC), Roman mosaics and Islamic art from Córdoba's heyday around the turn of the first millennium. *Tue*

Proud and charming – a flamenco dancer

informative view of the life of Muslims, Christians and Jews at the time of the Caliphate. A picture-postcard view can be enjoyed from here over the Guadalquivir and the *Puente Romano* – the Roman bridge built on foundations from the reign of Emperor Augustus – and the Mezquita. *May–Sept daily 10am–2pm, 4.30pm–8.30pm, Oct–April 10am–6pm | admission 4.50 euros*

FOOD & DRINK

INSIDER TIP AMALTEA
Modern Mediterranean fare and – a rarity in Andalucía – delicious salads. On the road along the banks of the Guadalquivir. *Closed Sun evening | tel. 9 57 49 19 68 | Ronda de Isasa 10 | www.amaltea.es | Budget–Moderate*

BODEGAS CAMPOS
Founded as a wine cellar in 1908 it is now a labyrinthine restaurant set around several courtyards. Exquisite Córdoba cuisine. *Closed Sun evening | C/Los Lineros 32 | tel. 9 57 49 75 00 | Expensive*

CASA PEPE DE LA JUDERÍA
Traditional food and very good tapas in cosy surroundings. *Daily | C/Romero 1 | tel. 9 57 20 07 44 | Moderate–Expensive*

EL CHURRASCO ●
Antiques gives this restaurant close to the Mezquita its special atmosphere. Steaks from cattle reared in the Valle de los Pedroches are very popular. *C/Romero 16 | tel. 9 57 29 08 19 | www.elchurrasco.com | Expensive*

SHOPPING

The *Zoco Municipal*, a market hall for hand-crafted products opposite the synagogue, looks like a tourist trap at first glance, but it isn't! Filigree silverwork, for which Córdoba is famous, can be found in the *Joyería Maimónides (Calle Romero 5)*. The locals head for the *Cordobán Meryan* workshops *(Calleja de las Flores 2)* for leather goods. The *Calle Cardenal González*, below the Mezquita, with its lovely boutiques, is an alternative to the souvenir shops in the Jewish Quarter.

LEISURE

HAMMAM BAÑOS ÁRABES ●
This hamam is considered one of the most beautiful of its kind. Arabian-inspired spa oasis with hot pools and massages. *Entry*

every two hours 10am–10pm | admission 23 euros, with massage 33 euros | C/ Corregidor Luis de la Cerda 51 | tel. 9 57 48 47 46 | www.hammamalandalus.com

ENTERTAINMENT

The new lounge/night café *Sojo Ribera* on the roof of the multi-storey car park *La Herradura* is smart and 'in'. *(Paseo de la Ribera 1 | at the Miraflores bridge over the Guadalquivir)*. Equally chic and especially cool is the new gastro bar INSIDER TIP *Fusion*, just a few yards further down the street on the corner of the Plaza del Potro. Lively pubs in the Old Town can be found on the *Plaza de la Corredera* and *Avda. Gran Capitán* near San Hipólito church. ● Good flamenco shows are held in *Tablao Cardenal (Feb–Nov Mon–Sat 10.30pm | admission 20 euros | C/Torrijos 10)*. On summer evenings INSIDER TIP flamenco concerts with well-known musicians can be enjoyed in the inner courtyard of the *Palacio Episcopal*. In the winter, a vaulted hall inside the palace is used.

WHERE TO STAY

ALBUCASIS
Welcoming 2-star hotel unusually located in the Judería district. *15 rooms | C/Buen Pastor 11 | tel. 9 57 47 86 25 | www.hotel albucasis.com | Budget–Moderate*

INSIDER TIP CASA DE LOS AZULEJOS
Beautifully furnished rooms in a building from colonial days with an attractive library. Near the Roman ruins and the Town Hall. *8 rooms | Fernando Colón 5 | tel. 9 57 47 00 00 | www.casadelosazulejos.com | Moderate*

HACIENDA POSADA DE VALLINA
Perfectly situated – near the Mezquita and yet in a quiet side street. Classically

and comfortably furnished rooms, if a bit small. *21 rooms | C/Corregidor Luis de la Cerda 83 | tel. 9 57 49 87 50 | www.hh posadadevallina.es | Moderate*

HOSPES PALACIO DEL BAILÍO
Córdoba's most beautiful hotel is on the northern edge of the Old Town. The palace complex with a romantic, contemporary interior, encloses four atmospheric *patios. 53 rooms | Ramírez de las Casas Deza 10–12 | tel. 9 57 49 89 93 | www. hospes.es | Expensive*

MAESTRE
A hotel with a hostel nearby. Pleasant atmosphere. *46 rooms | C/Romero Barros 4/6 | tel. 9 57 47 24 10 | www.hotel maestre.com | Budget*

INFORMATION

OFICINA DE TURISMO
C/Rey Heredia 22 | tel. 9 57 20 17 74; Turismo de Andalucía | C/Torrijos 10 (opposite the Mezquita) | tel. 9 57 35 51 79 | www.turismo decordoba.org
Other information stands can be found in the station, on the Plaza de las Tendillas and at the Alcázar.

WHERE TO GO

ALMODÓVAR DEL RÍO
(139 D4) (*ꬵ F–G 3*)
This beautiful, labyrinthine little town in the Guadalquivir valley (pop. 8000, 25km/ 15½mi west of Córdoba) is dominated by a massive, crenellated Moorish fortress dating from the 12th century *(Mon–Fri 11am–2.30pm, 4pm–8pm (in winter 7pm), Sat–Sun 11am–8pm (in winter 7pm) | admission 6.50 euros | www.castillode almodovar.com)*. Good food can be found in the restaurant *La Taberna (closed Mon, in July also Sun | C/Antonio Machado 24 |*

tel. 9 57 71 36 84 | www.latabernadealmo
dovardelrio.com | Moderate).

MADINAT AL-ZAHRA ⭐
(139 D4) (ØØ G3)

The Emir of Córdoba, Abd Ar Rahman III of the Umayyad dynasty felt powerful enough to claim the title Caliph for himself in 929. As a demonstration of his strength he ordered a new seat of parliament to be built beyond the gates of Córdoba – the Madinat al-Zahra (also known as the *Medina Azahara*). A fairy-tale palace-city was erected 10km (6¼mi) west of Córdoba. Word of its extravagant luxury soon spread around the world. However, tension within the new Caliphate led to this newly completed splendour being destroyed by forces opposed to the Umayyad dynasty in

1010. Excavation of the site started in 1911. Two buildings have been partially rebuilt and give some idea of the magnificent structures lost – the *Salón Rico* or the *Salón de Abd Ar Rahman III* and the *Edifício Basilical Superior*. Visits start at the new information and research centre where, apart from watching an informative film, you can marvel at selected finds in the purpose-built museum. A stop at the INSIDERTIP▶ museum shop which sells international literature on Spain's Muslim history is well worthwhile. A shuttle bus runs from the car park *(2.10 euros)* every 30 mins. to the excavation site that is located a little further up the hill. *May–mid Sept Tue–Sat 10am–8.30pm, Sun 10am–2pm, mid Sept–April Tue–Sat 10am–6.30pm, Sun 10am–2pm | free admis-*

More than 1000 years old – the Caliph's palace Medina Azahara near Córdoba

sion for EU citizens | special busses from Córdoba run daily at 10am, 11am and once in the afternoon | 7.20 euros | Depart from Avda. Alcázar and Paseo de la Victoria | tickets: tel. 9 02 20 17 74 or from the tourist information office near the station on the Plaza de las Tendillas or on the Campo Santo de los Mártires.

INSIDER TIP ▶ SIERRA SUBBÉTICA
(139 F5–6) (ꓳ H4)

The men of *Zuheros* (pop. 800) gather on the ⚜ Plaza de la Paz below the castle dating from the 9th century and look out over the olive groves and the surrounding *campiña* at their feet. The completely white village clings to the hillside of the Sierra Subbética, a fascinating, barren, mountainous area some distance from the

main road linking Córdoba and Granada that most tourists generally pass by. Those in a hurry miss out on dreamy villages like *Zuheros* and *Luque* and the surprisingly elaborate Baroque buildings along the *Ruta del Barroco*. The main town in the Sierra Subbética is *Priego de Córdoba* (pop. 23,500, 104km/65mi southeast of Córdoba) which boasts a white Old Town perched romantically on a rocky plateau. The cosy restaurant *El Aljibe (closed Mon | C/Abad Palomino 7 | tel. 9 57 70 18 56 | Budget–Moderate)* lies in the shadow of the Arabian fortress. Not far from there, among the tangle of narrow alleyways in the Old Town, is one of the nicest guest-houses in the area – *La Posada Real (7 rooms | C/Real 14 | tel. 9 57 54 19 10 | www.laposadareal.com | Budget)*. The very best, organic, extra native olive oil can be found at ☺ *Vizcántar (Ctra. Zagrilla | Priego de Córdoba)* and in Baena at *Núñez del Prado (Avda. de Cervantes 15)*. The oil mills are open to the public. On the northern edge of the Sierra is the *Vía Verde de la Subbética (see p. 109)* cycle route that follows the course of a former railway line. Informa-tion: *Oficina de Turismo (Plaza de la Constitución 3 | tel. 9 57 70 06 25 | www.turismodepriego.com)*

HUELVA

(136 B4) (ꓳ B5) This provincial capital (pop. 149,000) looks back on a history that is almost as long as that of Cádiz. Columbus set sail on his voyages of dis-covery from Palos de la Frontera.

Huelva is the commercial hub of the west-ern Costa de la Luz. During the Franco dictatorship Huelva was made into a centre of the petrochemical industry. The fishing fleet and the strawberry planta-tions in the surrounding area are also important economic factors. The city is

The lively Plaza de las Monjas in Huelva

pleasant, lively and surprisingly normal having lost its important sites of interest in the earthquake of 1755 that also razed Lisbon to the ground.

Some will find it a pleasant change to be away from the usual tourist routes as the surrounding area here has a completely different character than the eastern part of Andalucía. The virtually untouched dunes and the marshland *(marisma)* in the Coto de Doñana National Park are unique. And Palos de la Frontera played an important part in world history. It was from this former fishing village that Columbus set out for America on his first voyage of discovery. Sandy beaches, stretching for miles, follow the coastline.

SIGHTSEEING

BARRIO REINA VICTORIA

To the north of the centre, between the avenues *Alcalde Federico Molina* and *Guatemala*, is the architecturally interesting former British workers' settlement, Reina Victoria, built in 1917 by the *Riotinto* mining company.

FOOD & DRINK

PORTICHUELO

In the city centre, near the Gran Teatro. This restaurant is well known for its plain but very good food. Perfect too for those not particularly hungry as the tapas are really excellent. *Closed Sun | C/Vázquez López 15 | tel. 9 59 24 57 68 | Moderate*

WHERE TO STAY

TARTESSOS

Although located right in the centre, this 4-star hotel is extremely quiet and comfortable. Good business facilities and a gym. Bikes available for hire; putting green. *100 rooms | Avda. Martín Alonso Pinzón 13 | tel. 9 59 28 27 11 | www.euro starstartessos.com | Moderate*

INFORMATION

OFICINA DE TURISMO

Plaza Alcalde Coto Mora 2 | tel. 9 59 65 02 00; Plaza de las Monjas | tel. 9 59 25 12 18 | www.turismohuelva.org

WHERE TO GO

AYAMONTE (136 A4) (*III A5*)

The galleries of the old warehouses along the banks of the Río Guadiana are a reminder of the times when goods were ferried to and from Portugal by ship. Nowadays almost everything goes by motorway across the long suspension bridge over the river. The proximity to Portugal can be felt in the narrow, traffic-free lanes in the pretty town centre (pop. 20,000; 50km/31mi west of Huelva). The people of Vila Real opposite like coming over for a shop. The ☀ terrace at the modern *Parador de Ayamonte (Avda. de la Constitución | tel. 9 59 32 07 00 | www.parador.es | Moderate)* offers a lovely view of the town and estuary. *Casa Barberi (Paseo de la Ribera 12 | 9 59 47 02 89 | Moderate)* has been open to guests since 1917 and serves delicious fish and rice dishes. Both locals and visitors have to go 7km (4½mi) to the *Urbanisation Isla Canela* for a swim. When designing the hotels and blocks of flats an effort was made to avoid the monotony so typical of artificially planned resorts. The main attraction, however, is without doubt the vast beach and the sandbank that stretches right out into the sea. Information: *Oficina de Turismo (C/Huelva 27 | tel. 9 5 93 20 73)*

PALOS DE LA FRONTERA AND THE COLUMBUS ROUTE (136 B4) (*III B5*)

Christopher Columbus (or Cristóbal Colón in Spanish) set out on his first voyage of discovery on 3 August, 1492, from this village of whitewashed houses at the mouth of the Río Tinto (13km/8mi southeast of Huelva). This journey was to take him westwards in search of a passage to India. The last church service before sailing was held at the *Iglesia San Jorge*. The ship lay at anchor a little down river. Having silted up, the harbour no longer exists.

After fleeing Portugal in 1485 the first place the native of Genoa sought out was the *Monasterio de La Rábida (Tue–Sat 10.30am–1pm, 4pm–6.15pm, July–19 Aug 8pm, Sun 10.45am–1pm | admission 3 euros)*. Accompanied by his son, it was here that he knocked on the gates, totally exhausted. And it was here that he later planned his first voyage.

An alabaster statue of the Virgin Mary (14th century) is noteworthy. Columbus discussed his plans with the padres in the chapter house. The botanical gardens *Jardín Botánico José Celestino Mutis* which boasts plants from the Iberian peninsula and Latin America is at the foot of the hill. The main attractions in the *Muelle de las Carabelas (June–Sept Tue–Fri 10am–2pm, 5pm–9pm, Sat and Sun 11am–8pm, Oct–May Tue–Sun 10am–7pm | admission 3.55 euros | www.turismohuelva.org)* are the replicas of Columbus' three ships. A medieval village and several Indians' huts set the period scene while the main building contains maps and information boards with facts about Columbus' three voyages.

Accommodation is available in the neighbouring village *Moguer*, a *pueblo blanco*, that lies on the Columbus Route. The pleasant country hotel *Plaza Escribano (20 rooms | tel. 9 59 37 30 63 | C/Lora Tamayo 5 | www.hotelplazaescribano.com | Budget)* is built around three *patios*.

PARQUE NACIONAL COTO DE DOÑANA ★ (137 D5–6) (*III C5*)

One of the most important areas of natural beauty in Europe lies in the Guadalquivir delta (65km/40mi east of Huelva) – the Coto de Doñana National Park. Permanently flooded swathes of land, the *marismas,* behind huge migrating dunes, provide an ideal environment for more than 300 types of bird, ranging from the purple heron to the pied avocet.

Over an area of some 210mi² nature is left to its own accord. The imperial eagle and the Iberian lynx have also found refuge here. For centuries the Doñana was the hunting ground *(coto)* of the powerful, until biologists drew attention the region's unprecedented ecological importance in the 1950s. It has been a national park since 1969 and was declared a Unesco World Heritage Site in 1994. In 1998, a holding dam upriver from the park burst, releasing poisonous mine tailings into the river and polluting the river Guadiamar that flows through the Doñana over a length of 50km (31mi).

The peace and quiet of the Doñana is interrupted twice a day by the thunder of 4×4 buses bumping visitors around the southern part of the park. This thrilling 4-hour excursion is well worth the ride *(May–mid Sept Mon–Sat 8.30am, 5pm, mid Sept–April Tue–Sun 8.30am, 3pm | fare 29.50 euros | departing from the Acebuche visitor centre on the western edge of the park | tel. 9 59 43 04 32). The information centre (www.donanavisitas. es | www.donana.es) is open daily 8am–7pm. Other visitor centres are La Rocina (A 483, at km 16) and Centro de Visitantes Palacio del Acebrón (A 83, at km 16). Both open daily in summer 9am–3pm, 4pm–9pm, otherwise 7pm*. Hiking trails lead into the peripheral areas of the national park.

INSIDER TIP ▶ PLAYA DE MAZAGÓN
(136 C5) (*ω B5*)

The holiday resort *Matalascañas* was conjured out of nowhere at the end of the 1960s in the southwestern corner of the present Doñana National Park on the Costa de la Luz.

In the *Parque Dunar* on the outskirts heading out to Mazagón the *Museo del Mundo Marino* provides a clear overview of life in and with the sea. *(At present the*

BOOKS & FILMS

▶ **The Hand of Fatima** – This almost 1000 page tome by the internationally successful author Ildefonso Falcones takes the reader back to the Kingdom of Granada in 16th-century Andalucía

▶ **The Ignorance of Blood** – Robert Wilson's psychological thriller from 2009 takes the reader on a journey to Sevilla with his famous inspector Jefe Javier Falcón. The city is in the aftermath of a terrorist attack and a dead gangster and a suitcase full of banknotes suggest that Falcón has the dangerous Russian mafia on his hands

▶ **Winter in Lisbon** – By Antonio Muñoz Molina is a homage to the genres of film noir and jazz music. Other works by the contemporary Andalucían writer include *Sepharad*

▶ **Knight and Day** – An action comedy film partly filmed in Andalucía. Tom Cruise and Cameron Diaz charge around the Old Towns of Cádiz and Sevilla (USA 2010)

▶ **Lawrence of Arabia** – Is just one of the many blockbusters filmed in part in Andalucía. Others include *Cleopatra*, *Doctor Zhivago* and *Indiana Jones and the Last Crusade*

Spain's most important wetlands – the Coto de Doñana National Park

museum is closed due to lack of funds. For more information please contact the tourist information centre on the Avda. de las Adelfas, Matalascañas | www.parque dunar.es).

Those wanting to avoid mass tourism in Spain can find a virtually untouched sandy beach 23km (14½mi) long and up to 120m wide, just a little bit further west, between Matalascañas and Mazagón. It is uniquely located at the foot of a sandy cliff more than 100m (328ft) high along the edge of a migrating dune that has since become static.

The beach is reached via a 1200m-long boardwalk across the dunes from *Cuesta Maneli car park (off the A494 at km 39)* or via the approach road to the Parador in Mazagón (20km/12½mi) southeast of Huelva).

The lovely *Parador (63 rooms | Ctra. A494, at km 30 | tel. 9 59 53 63 00 | www.parador. es | Expensive)* just a little way outside Mazagón was built at the end of the 1960s in the middle of a pine forest on a hillside overlooking the sea.

EL ROCÍO (137 D5) (⌀ C5)

This famous place of pilgrimage (pop. 1600, 65km/40mi east of Huelva) has a Wild West feel to it thanks to the sandy paths and wooden verandas. The golden garments of the Virgen del Rocío are in stark contrast to the plain, white-painted church. The first chapel was built here at the end of the 13th century to honour the 'Virgin of the Dew'. The present shrine dates from 1961. Some 100 holy brotherhoods *(hermandades)* make the pilgrimage to El Rocío at Whitsun, accompanied by up to one million others. Just beyond the village, flamingos can be seen wading through the *marismas*.

Good regional cooking at moderate prices is available in the restaurant *Toruño (closed Tue | Plaza del Acebuchal s/n | tel. 9 59 44 24 22 | Moderate)*.

The hotel of the same name, built in the typical El Rocío village style, is next door *(30 rooms | Plaza del Acebuchal 22 | tel. 9 59 44 23 23 | www.toruno.es | Moderate, considerably more expensive at Whitsun | advance booking essential)*.

Horses and carriages in front of the white pilgrimage church in El Rocío

SEVILLA

▓▓▓ **MAP INSIDE BACK COVER**
▓▓▓ (137 E4) *(ᐧ D4)*
Youths on mopeds in jeans and T-shirts wind their way between the traffic on the Avenida de la Constitución.

The never-ending rattle of two-stroke engines is one of the many sounds typical to this city, like trotting horses, flamenco music blaring out of loudspeakers in bars and the long drawn-out call of blind lottery-ticket sellers. This city with a population of 700,000 – the fourth largest after Madrid, Barcelona and Valencia – is bursting with life. However, the Sevillians are never hectic. The sun, shining a merciless white at midday and bathing the streets in a reddish hue in the evenings, curbs any restlessness. A labyrinth of narrow streets and squares, with monuments, lush gardens and blocks of flats crowned by roof terraces can be found around the Giralda – originally a minaret and converted into a bell tower for the cathedral – now one of the city's major landmarks. *Sevilla* experienced its heyday under the rule of the Berber Almohad dynasty at the turn of the first millennium and a good 500 years later when caught up in the fever of discovery and the exploitation of Latin America. But the city does not live from its great past alone. The world's attention was focused on Sevilla during the Expo 1992 for which a new district was created on the peninsula La Cartuja. This is also where the biennale for contemporary art (BIACS) has been held since 2004. An underground railway system was been in operation below the ancient streets since 2009 while, above ground, the Sevillians have discovered the pleasure of cycling thanks to the practical bike hire scheme. Beyond the city boundary, a ☺ revolutionary thermosolar plant feeds

energy from the sun into the electricity network. Things are on the go in Sevilla – and this can be seen in the cool bars and trendy boutiques found in *La Macarena* or the *Triana* district, and in the number of young tourists who are drawn to the regional capital.

CITY WHERE TO START?
City centre: Get your bearings from the Giralda and the cathedral. This is where you will find the Reales Alcázares, the Archive of the Indies and Barrio Santa Cruz with its many tapas bars. From here the Guadalquivir and Torre de Oro are not far. Drivers should head for one of the multi-storeys – the one on Paseo Colón is easy to find. The bus route C5 and tramline 1 pass close to the cathedral.

SIGHTSEEING

ARCHIVO GENERAL DE INDIAS
After Columbus set sail in the name of the Spanish crown in 1492, hoping to find a new passage to India via a western route and accidentally discovering America in the process, Sevilla developed into a trade centre between the New and the Old Worlds. The discovery of America and trading between the continents is documented in the General Archive of the Indies. *Mon–Sat 9.30am–4.45pm, Sun 10am–2pm | admission free | Plaza del Triunfo*

AYUNTAMIENTO
The 16th-century town hall, as seen from Plaza San Francisco, is a magnificent example of late Gothic architecture in Spain, whereas its main façade on Plaza Nueva is in a plain neo-Classical style following the building's extension. *Guided tours Sept–July Tue–Thu 5.30pm, 6pm, Sat 12 noon | admission free*

BARRIO SANTA CRUZ ★
Spend a few hours wandering around this fairy-tale suburb in the shadow of the Reales Alcázares – head off without a map and explore the narrow streets of whitewashed houses, stop for a cup of coffee in one of the bars or visit the little shops. The loveliest of the many squares is not actually a square at all – in the *Calle Lope de Rueda* potted plants turn the road into a cosy courtyard perfect for locals to meet for a chat. The Jewish Quarter was the scene of a pogrom in 1391 and the expulsion of its residents in 1492.

CASA DE PILATOS ●
The House of Pontius Pilate is a fantastic city palace that was built at the end of the 16th century in the Mudéjar style. *April–Oct daily 9am–7pm, Nov–March daily 9am–6pm | admission 6 euros (ground*

floor only), 8 euros (whole palace), free
Wed 3pm–7pm | Plaza de Pilatos

CATEDRAL AND GIRALDA ⭐

'Let us build a church so beautiful and so
great that those who see it built will think
we were mad.' This target set by a mem-
ber of the cathedral chapter was taken
up by the builders of Sevilla cathedral
(15th century) who erected the largest
Gothic ecclesiastical building in the world.
The sarcophagus just inside the south
door, supported by four bearers sculpted
in stone, has housed Columbus' mortal
remains since 1902. That they really are
the remains of the explorer was con-
firmed by DNA tests in 2006. The skeleton
is, however, not complete. The highlight
in the interior of the building is the high
altar with its dizzying wealth of ornamentation that took 100 years to complete.
Like almost everywhere in Andalucía the
cathedral was built on the site of a mosque
of which the orange tree courtyard and
the ☘ Giralda, a minaret from the 12th
century, still exist. While being converted
into a bell tower in the 16th century, the
minaret was given a Renaissance-style
spire, crowned with a 4m (13ft)-high figure holding a standard and a palm twig
in its hands. This Giraldillo turns in the
wind (girar is Spanish for 'to turn') and
lent its name to the whole tower that is
97m (318ft) high. The tip of the Giralda
can be reached up a sloping ramp and
offers the best views over the old part of
Sevilla. Mon–Sat 11am–5.30pm (July/Aug
9.30am–4.30pm), Sun 2.30pm–6.30pm |
admission cathedral and Giralda 8 euros |
www.catedraldesevilla.es

HOSPITAL DE LA CARIDAD

In the 17th century Sevillian artists, including Murillo and Valdés Leal, painted a
series of remarkable works for the Charity
Hospital on the transcience of being.

Mon–Thu 9am–7pm, Fri/Sat 9am–1pm,
3.30pm–7pm, Sun 9am–1pm | admission
5 euros | C/Temprado 3

ISLA LA CARTUJA

The Sevillians held their celebrated Expo
in 1992 on the 'Island of the Charterhouse'.
Where once the Expo lake was, is now the
leisure park Isla Mágica. The Puente del
Alamillo, one of the distinctive bridges
designed by the Spanish star architect
Santiago Calatrava, spans the Guadalquivir
a little to the north of the park like a huge
harp. To the south is the former Charterhouse monastery Monasterio de Santa
María de las Cuevas, which now houses
the Andalucían contemporary art centre
Centro Andaluz de Arte Contemporáneo
(Tue–Sat 11am–8pm, April–Sept 11am–
9pm, Sun all year round 11am–3pm | ad-
mission 3 euros, Tue free admission for
EU citizens | www.caac.es). South of the
Puente de la Cartuja (Camino de los Des-
cubrimientos 2 | Tue–Sat 10am–7.30pm,
summer 8.30pm, Sun all year round 10am–
3pm | admission 4.90 euros | www.pabel
londelanavegacion.es) is the 50m (164ft)-
high tower Pabellón de la Navegación.
Tickets for the maritime museum include
access to the viewing platform.

METROPOL PARASOL

This huge structure on the Plaza de la
Encarnación provides shade and houses
a central market and viewing terraces.
The Sevillians christened this sculptural
design by the German architect Jürgen
Mayer H. Las Setas – the mushrooms. A
lift links the lower levels with the restaurant and viewing areas, from which a
☘ winding walkway 20m (66ft) above
the ground offers superb views of the
Old Town. During construction work, the
remains of walls from the Roman period
were uncovered. Visitors can walk around
the ruins of Ancient Sevilla dating from

The Giralda, the former 12th-century minaret towers over the cathedral in Sevilla

between 30–400AD in the underground Antiquarium museum. *Mon–Thu 10.30am–midnight, Fri, Sat 1am | admission 1.35 euros | Plaza de la Encarnación 35 | www.metropolsevilla.com*

MUSEO ARQUEOLÓGICO

The Archaeological Museum, housed in one of the pavilions used for the Ibero-American Exposition of 1929, is famous for finds from Itálica, the Roman settlement in the northwest of Sevilla and the Treasure of El Carambolo from the 8th and 7th centuries BC. *Tue–Sat 9am–8.30pm, Sun 9am–2.30pm | free admission for EU citizens | Plaza de América*

MUSEO DEL BAILE FLAMENCO

This historical town house in the *barrio* Santa Cruz provides a multimedia look at the history of the flamenco. Regular events on anything to do with the flamenoc are

held as well as flamenco courses. *Museum daily 9.30am–7pm, flamenco shows daily from 7pm | Calle Manuel Rojas Marcos 3 | admission 10 euros | www.museoflamenco.com*

MUSEO DE BELLAS ARTES ●

The magnificent museum of fine art is located in a 17th-century monastery. The focus is on Spanish painting from the 17th and 18th centuries. The museum boasts treasures from the Sevilla School, including works by Zurbarán, Murillo and Valdés Leal. *Tue–Sat 9am–8.30pm, Sun 9am–2.30pm | free admission for EU citizens | Plaza del Museo 9*

PLAZA DE ESPAÑA

Just a short walk to the south of the heart of the Old Town brings you to the ● *Parque de María Luisa* that was laid out for the Ibero-American Exposition of 1929.

The Plaza de España lies rather artificially like a film set right in the middle of the park, with an imposing, semi-circular building with a diameter of 200m (656ft) at one end. The outer walls are covered with decorative tiles depicting scenes from the history of the Spanish provinces. The benches below are perfect for lazying around.

REALES ALCÁZARES ★ ●

The royal palace complex can be a bit confusing to visitors at first. It was not Arabs who had these buildings constructed but the Christian King Peter the Cruel (14th century). He created a distinctly royal nest for himself and his lover, María de Padilla. However, the builders were Moors, sent by rulers of the Nasrid dynasty from Granada. The result is the most beautiful building in the Mudéjar style anywhere – a fairy tale from 'One Thousand and One Nights'. Between playful Arabian ornamentation there are numerous symbols of Catholic Spain – the castle and the lion – as well as the motto of the Nasrid kings in Arabic script: 'There is no victor but Allah'. One highlight inside is the *Sala de Embajadores* (Hall of the Ambassadors) with its richly decorated vaulted ceiling. A visit to the gardens of the Reales Alcázares alone is well worthwhile. They are a scented island of tranquillity with fountains and tiled benches plumb in the middle of the city.

The atmospheric INSIDER TIP 'Alcázar Nights', with concerts after 10.30pm and a bar, run from July until mid September. Tickets costing 4 euros have to be bought during the day at the Alcázar. *April–Sept daily 9.30am–7pm, Oct–March daily 9.30am–5pm | admission 8.75 euros | www.patronato-alcazarsevilla.es*

REAL MAESTRANZA BULLRING

Sevilla's 18th-century Plaza de Toros seating 14,000 is the largest in Andalucía and the most important in Spain outside Madrid. *Daily 9.30am–7pm, May–Oct 9.30am–8pm, on days bullfights are held*

Colourful tiled pictures on the Plaza de España

9.30am–3pm | admission 7 euros | Plaza de Toros | www.realmaestranza.com

TORRE DEL ORO

The golden tower on the banks of the Guadalquivir was built as a defensive tower around 1220 under the Moors. Sevilla's second most famous landmark after the Giralda was originally covered with gilded ceramic tiles. The Torre del Oro now houses the maritime museum. *Mon–Fri 9.30am–6.45pm, Sat/Sun 10.30am–6.45pm | admission 3 euros*

TRIANA

The residents of the district to the west of the Guadalquivir live in a world of their own. From their point of view Sevilla is, at best, merely an important area the other side of the river. Triana boasts the city's oldest church, the *Iglesia de Santa Ana* (1280). A visit to this part of town can be recommended for its nightlife and craft shops.

FOOD & DRINK

It is really a bit of a shame to spend the evening in just one restaurant. So do as the Sevillians do and go on a tapas tour. A good place to start is the area around the *Museo de Bellas Artes*, Alfalfa and San Salvador squares and the *barrio Santa Cruz*, in particular. One bar next to another can be found in the *Calle Mateos*. The *Cervecería Giralda (Mateos Gago 1 | closed Sun)* is a classic. The bar *Las Teresas (Santa Teresa 2)* in Santa Cruz has been around for 150 years – quite unaffected by the streams of tourist.

El Rinconcillo has successfully kept its authentic charm in the face of all the trends in the worlds of fashion and design. The tapas bar at *Calle Gerona 40*, reputedly the oldest in the whole of Andalucía, has been serving wine from southern Spain

ever since 1670. The tapas in **INSIDER TIP** *Vinería San Telmo (Paseo Catalina de Ribera 4)* will satisfy any gourmet. The well-run, old-fashioned bar *Hijos Morales (García de Vinuesa 11)* between the cathedral and La Maestranza is also well worth a visit. If you fancy a snack or a break when shopping in the city centre head for the bar *Patio San Eloy (C/San Eloy 9)* where you sit with your plate on a tiered seating area, like a grandstand. The charming café/cake shop *La Campana (C/Sierpes 1)* with its sweet delicacies is always inviting.

INSIDER TIP ALBARAMA

Who would have though that you could eat so well and in such pleasantly stylish surroundings bang in the middle of the city? The mini tuna burgers on bread with sesame seeds or the tapas creations with foie gras and slithers of apple in Pedro Ximenes sherry are delicious. *Closed Sun evenings | Plaza San Francisco 5 | tel. 9 54 22 97 84 | www.restaurantealbarama. com | Moderate*

INSIDER TIP LOS ALCORES

Popular *mesón* (rustic restaurant) in Triana. This is where you can eat like the locals – plain cooking using the best, fresh ingredients. *Closed Mon | C/Farmacéutico Murillo Herrera 10 | tel. 9 54 27 06 61 | Budget*

AZ-ZAIT

Small, exquisite gourmet restaurants like Az-Zait are a rarity in Sevilla. The décor however is rather kitschy. Excellent Andalucían fare at a reasonable price. *Closed Sun | Plaza San Lorenzo 1 | tel. 9 54 90 64 75 | Moderate–Expensive*

TABERNA DEL ALABARDERO

Modern Andalucían cooking in a 19th-century town palace. Luxurious. Also offers affordable lunches. *Daily | C/Zaragoza 20 | tel. 9 54 50 27 21 | Expensive*

SHOPPING

Sevilla's main shopping area is around the *Calle Sierpes* and *Calle Tetuán* to the north of the town hall; Victorio & Lucchino, Sevilla's internationally famous fashion designers, can be found at *Calle Sierpes 87*. The traditional art of the *abanico*, the fan, can be marvelled at nos. 70 and 75 where a large selection is on view. Crafted items can be found in Triana on and around the streets *Alfarería, Antillano* and *San Jorge*.

A good selection of historical *azulejos* – tiles – at moderate prices is available at **INSIDER TIP** *Cerámicas Antonio del Rey Fernández (C/Feria 15)*. From here, a quick detour to the **INSIDER TIP** *Corral de Artesanos (C/Castellar 52)*, a hidden courtyard where statues of the Virgin Mary and floats for Easter processions are carved, is a must.

Culinary delicacies can be enjoyed, for example, at *Patí tó (C/Arrayán 23)* very close to the city's most beautiful market hall on *Calle Feria* in the *La Macarena* district. A delightful flea market is held in the *Calle Feria* every Thursday morning where you can find everything from pets to antiques.

FLAMENCO COURSES

Sevilla is the flamenco capital. Lots of dancing schools run courses for visitors and tourists, e.g. ● *Carmen de Torres (Lepanto 7 | www.flamenco-carmendetorres.com)* or the ● *Flamenco Centre (Peral 49 | www.tallerflamenco.com)*.

ENTERTAINMENT

Sevilla is famous for its nightlife. People of all ages spend the mild evenings in the bars on *Mateos Gago*, right next to the Giralda, or in Triana, around the *Puente Isabel II* and on the *Calle Betis*. The young congregate in the evenings in the city centre between *Alfalfa* and *Salvador* squares (e.g. in the pub *Sopa de Ganso*) or in the *Arenal* district to the west of the *Avenida de la Constitución*.

The pubs in the *Alameda de Hércules* attract the non-mainstream crowd. In July and August the terraces on the *Plaza América* in the Parque María Luisa and the banks of the Guadalquivir below the square are very popular.

The most chichi club in Triana is **INSIDER TIP** *Boss (C/Betis 67 | closed Sun–Tue | www.salaboss.es)*. The 'in' crowd go to the open-air disco on the Isla de la Cartuja. *Antique (Tue–Sat midnight–7am | C/Matemáticos Rey Pastor y Castro s/n)*.

A number of *tablaos* offer flamenco shows for tourists. The most commendable are *Los Gallos (daily 8pm, 10.30pm | admission 30 euros | Plaza Santa Cruz 11 | tel. 9 54 21 69 81 | www.tablaolosgallos.com)* and *El Arenal (daily 8pm, 10pm | admission from 36 euros incl. a drink | C/Rodo 7 | tel. 9 54 21 64 92 | www.tablaoelarenal.com)*. There are also two pubs that sometimes have flamenco shows that are not just for tourists: *Casa Anselma (Mon–Sat 11.30pm–3am | C/Pagés del Corro 49)* in Triana and the old classic – but often packed to bursting point – *La Carbonería (daily 20pm–3.30am | C/Levíes 18 | tel. 9 54 21 44 60)* north of the *barrio* Santa Cruz. You will enjoy an evening here on days when there are no performances too.

WHERE TO STAY

Most hotels in Sevilla increase their prices during Semana Santa and the Feria de Abril, even charging double the price.

A local pub in the *barrio* Santa Cruz

ALFONSO XIII

One of the most elegant hotels in all of Spain. Built in the Mudéjar style in 1928 and renovated in 2012. Even just a cup of coffee in the hotel bar looking into the *patio* is a treat. *147 rooms | C/San Fernando 2 | tel. 9 54 91 70 00 | www. hotel-alfonsoxiii-seville.com | Expensive*

INSIDER TIP ▶ AMADEUS

This small hotel in the former Jewish Quarter boasts not only individually furnished rooms but guests can rent musical instruments and practice in the music room or book one of the sound-proofed rooms with a piano. *14 rooms | Farnesio 6 | tel. 9 54 50 14 43 | www.hotelamadeus-sevilla.com | Moderate*

APARTMENTS METRÓPOLIS

Up to six people can stay in the pleasant and spacious penthouse flat with its own terrace. The other flats, furnished in a modern style, are equally inviting. Ideal for families or if staying for a longer period. Near the Museo de Bellas Artes. *C/ Bajeles 16–20 | tel. 9 55 54 28 21 | www. hostelsevillasuites.es | Budget*

CASA SACRISTÍA SANTA ANA

This romantic boutique hotel is located on the lively Alameda de Hércules and is arranged around an atmospheric *patio*. The neo-Baroque interior is definitely not for purists or minimalists. *25 rooms | Alameda de Hércules 22 | tel. 9 54 91 57 22 | www.hotelsacristia.com | Budget–Moderate*

LAS CASAS DE LA JUDERÍA

The hotel situated right next to the church Santa Maria La Blanca was originally 27 flats. Romantic *patios* link the various sections of the building. In summer, guests can enjoy the roof-top pool. *118 rooms | C/Santa María la Blanca 5 | tel. 9 54 41 51 50 | www.casasypalacios.com | Moderate–Expensive*

EME FUSION ●

The new, luxury boutique hotel opposite the cathedral spreads over 14 old town houses. Elegant, hip design. Four restaurants, a small spa area and a spectacular roof terrace. *63 rooms | C/Alemanes 5 | tel. 9 54 56 00 00 | www.emecatedralho-tel.com | Expensive*

PALACIO ALCÁZAR ☺

A charming boutique hotel just a few yards from the cathedral. The rooms are well sound-proofed and the whole building is, by Spanish standards, run on an energy-conscious, environmentally-friendly basis. *12 rooms | Plaza de la Alianza 11 | tel. 9 54 50 21 90 | www.hotelpalacioalcazar.com | Budget–Moderate*

INFORMATION

OFICINA DE TURISMO

Tourist information office for the city and region *(Avda. de la Constitución 21 B | tel. 9 54 78 75 78)*. Branches in the station and at the airport *(www.turismosevilla. org)*.
Other tourist offices in Sevilla: C/Arjona 28; Plaza de San Francisco 19; Paseo de las Delicias 9, tel.9 54 22 17 14 | www.visita sevilla.es. The 'Sevilla Card' and 'Sevilla Card Cultura' entitle holders to free entry to museums as well as other reductions *(1–3 days from 33 euros | www.sevillacard. es)*.

LOW BUDGET

▶ Bargain hunting – rummage around the flea market held every Thu in the Calle Feria (La Macarena) in Sevilla's Old Town.

▶ It's cheaper to buy *Jamón Ibérico de Bellota* where it is produced – namely in Aracena and Jabugo.

▶ A fantastic lunch can be had for just 13 euros in the elegant restaurant *La Taberna del Alabardero (C/Zaragoza 20 | tel. 9 54 50 27 21)* in Sevilla.

WHERE TO GO

CARMONA (138 B6) *(Ø E4)*

Every nook and cranny of this town (pop. 29,000, 38km/23½mi east of Sevilla) oozes history. You will come across countless reminders of Carthaginian, Roman, Moorish and medieval Christian influences on a stroll from the *Puerta de Sevilla* through the historic centre, across the *Plaza San Fernando* to the *Puerta de Córdoba*. Near the Puerta de Sevilla and the ruins of a 9th-century Moorish fortress is the ⭐ *Torre del Oro (Mon–Sat 10am–6pm, Sun 10am–3pm | admission 2 euros)* which offers panoramic views.
Of all the palaces and churches the *Iglesia de San Pedro* with its Giralda-like bell tower and the magnificent *Sagrario (near the Puerta de Sevilla)*, as well as the *Iglesia de Santa María (Plaza del Marqués de las Torres)* with its Moorish *patio*, are particularly noteworthy. Beyond the city boundary is the most important Roman cemetery in Spain – the *Necrópolis Romana (Tue–Fri 9am–6pm, Sat/Sun 9am–3.30pm, July/ Aug Tue–Fri 9am–2.30pm, 3pm–5.30pm, Sat/Sun 9am–3pm | free admission for EU citizens | Avda. Jorge Bónsor 9)*. Some tombs such as the *Tumba de Servilia* are like subterranean palaces.
Good regional cooking can be found at the *Restaurante San Fernando (closed Sun | C/Sacramento 3 | tel. 9 54 14 35 56 | Moderate)* on the *plaza* of the same name. One of the most beautiful Paradors in Spain has been created in the ● *Alcázar del Rey Don Pedro (63 rooms | tel. 9 54 14 10 10 | www.parador.es | Moderate– Expensive)*, built in the 14th century by Peter the Cruel, located in the eastern part of the Old Town. It is well worth a visit at least for a cup of coffee. Information: *Tourist information in the Puerta de Sevilla (tel. 9 54 19 09 55 | www.turismo. carmona.org)*

Itálica takes visitors back to Roman times

ITÁLICA ●

(137 E4) (*ΩD4*)

A stroll through the ruins of Andalucía's most important Roman settlement, Itálica, is a fascinating experience. Founded in 206BC, it is located 10km (6¼mi) northwest of Sevilla on the outskirts of *Santiponce*. It was here that the later emperors Trajan and Hadrian grew up in the 1st century AD. Itálica's demise followed the conquest of the Iberian peninsula by the Arabs. Excavations here began in the 18th century. One highlight of the visit is the *amphitheatre* that seats 25,000 and the *Casa del Planetario* with its well-preserved mosaic floors. *April–Sept Tue–Sat 8.30am–9pm, Sun 9am–3pm, Oct–March Tue–Sat 9am–6.30pm, Sun 10am–3pm | free admission for EU citizens | Avda. Extremadura 2 | Santiponce*

OSUNA (143 E1) (*ΩF5*)

The massive Renaissance church ☆ *La Colegiata (May–Sept daily 10am–1.30pm, 4pm–7pm, Oct–April daily 10am–1.30pm, 3.30pm–6.30pm, closed Sun afternoon in July/Aug | admission 3 euros)* towers above the little town (pop. 18,000), 91km (57mi) east of Sevilla. Its fortress-like façade conceals a light-filled interior with paintings by Ribera, among others. Osana was a university town from 1549–1820 and still radiates the glory of its past. Diagonally opposite the Colegiata is the *Convento de la Encarnación (Tue–Sun May–Sept 10am–1.30pm, 4pm–7pm, otherwise 10am–1.30pm, 3.30pm–6.30pm | admission 4 euros | Plaza de la Encarnación)* which now houses a museum of religious art. A highlight is a cycle of images on wall tiles from the 18th century. The archaeological museum in Torre de Agua is also well worth a visit. The restaurant *Casa Curro (closed Mon | Plaza Salitre 5 | tel. 9 55 82 07 58 | Budget)* is well known for its excellent regional fare – with more than 200 different tapas. The elegant hotel *El Palacio Marqués de la Gomera (20 rooms | C/San Pedro 20 | tel. 9 54 81 22 23 | www.hotelpalaciodelmarques.es | Budget–Moderate)*, in a Baroque palace, justifies any detour. Information: *Oficina de Turismo (Plaza Mayor | tel. 9 54 81 57 32 | www.turismosuna.es)*.

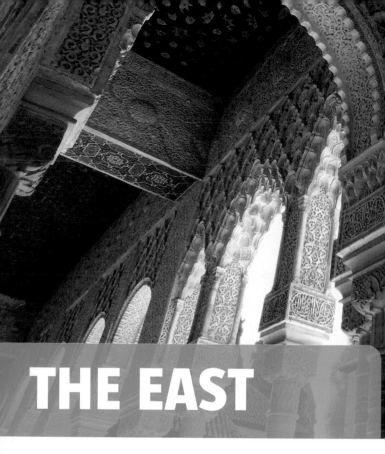

THE EAST

The east of Andalucía – the provinces Jaén, Granada and Almería – sometimes feels as if it has been forgotten by the rest of the region. Andalucía's capital, Sevilla, is a long way away, the infrastructure modest. Nevertheless visitors come here in droves to see the most exquisite architectural treasure from the Moorish period – the Alhambra in Granada.

There is however much more to be discovered. The Guadalquivir has its source in the Sierra de Cazorla (Jaén province) and, after a few twists and turns, flows towards Córdoba. Battalions of olive trees were planted along its banks, right up into the mountains themselves. Jaén can rightfully claim to be the world's olive oil capital. Further to the southeast the countryside is too barren even for the undemanding olive tree. The Altiplano in the eastern region of the provinces Granada and Almería is pure desert – incredibly fascinating to look at, but not to put a smile on the face of any environmentalist. Business-minded agriculturalists have turned the coast of Almería into a 'Costa del Plástico'. For miles on end the whole area is covered in plastic sheets, under which vegetables and fruit are ripened and harvested by immigrants from North Africa and Eastern Europe. To the east of Granada is the *Mulhacén*, at 3481m (11,420ft) the highest mountain

Photo: Ceiling in the Court of the Lions at the Alhambra, Granada

Moorish architectural wonders –
the Alhambra is just one of the fascinating
buildings surrounded by fantastic scenery

on the Iberian Peninsula, plumb in the middle of the Sierra Nevada which boasts a skiing area just 40km (25mi) from the beaches of the Costa Tropical.

ALMERÍA

(147 D5) (*N6*) **Although the provincial capital (pop. 190,000) cannot be com-** **pared to cities such as Sevilla, Granada or Córdoba, it is still very much worth visiting.**

The main attraction of this lively port is the fortress, the *Alcazaba*. The Old Town is dominated by the bulwark-like cathedral (16th century) which houses three paintings by the 17th-century artist Alonso Cano. The steel monstrosity in the harbour, *El Cable Inglés* (also called the

ALMERÍA

🏙 WHERE TO START?

Plaza de Estación: Anyone arriving by train or bus should cross the Plaza de Estación to the Gregorio Marañón bus stop, from where the no. 11 bus will take you to the historical city centre. Drivers should head for one of the multi-storey car parks nearby – there are two on the Avenida García Lorca. The Old Town is not far from here.

☀️ towers climb up the hill San Cristóbal (70m/230ft). *April–Oct Tue–Sun 9am–8.30pm, Nov–March Tue–Sun 9am–6.30pm | free admission for EU citizens*

FOOD & DRINK

CASA PUGA

A visit to this typically Andalucían bar alone would make a detour to Almería worthwhile. The many different types of tapas are simply incredible as is the wine list. It is hardly surprising that this bar,

View from the Moorish fortress Alcazaba with Almería far below

'English Bridge'), from which cargo was loaded onto ships from 1904 onwards, is now part of the city's industrial heritage.

SIGHTSEEING

ALCAZABA

The largest Moorish fortress in Spain was built on the orders of Abd ar Rahman III, the first Caliph of Córdoba, in 955. The three mighty curtain walls and their

founded in 1870, is still going strong. *Closed Sun | C/Jovellanos 7 | tel. 9 50 23 15 30 | www.barcasapuga.es | Budget–Moderate*

CASA SEVILLA

This pleasant restaurant is painted in warm shades of red both outside and in. Classic Andalucían fare is served which, although not unduly imaginative, is very good. Some 8000 different types of wine are stored in the cellar. *Closed Sun/Mon |*

C/Rueda López | Galería Comercial | tel. 9 50 27 29 12 | www.casa-sevilla.com | Moderate–Expensive

WHERE TO STAY

CATEDRAL

This 19th-century town house is centrally located next to the cathedral. Stylish, modern rooms. Small roof-top pool. *20 rooms | Plaza Catedral 8 | tel. 9 50 27 81 78 | www.hotelcatedral.net | Moderate*

TORRELUZ CENTRO

A 2-star hotel right in the middle of the Old Town. The 24 rooms are furnished in an unobtrusive modern style. If you fancy a bit more luxury and a pool, try the more expensive *Neuvo Torreluz* that was completely revamped in 2012. *Plaza Flores 8 | tel. 9 50 23 43 99 | www.torreluz.com | Budget*

INFORMATION

OFICINA DE TURISMO

Plaza de la Constitución | tel. 9 50 21 05 38 and *Parque Nicolás Salmerón (on the harbour promenade) | tel. 9 50 27 43 55 | www.almeria-turismo.org, www.turismodealmeria.org*

WHERE TO GO

CUEVAS DE SORBAS (147 E4) (ⓜ N5)

There are three guided routes through this fantastic cave system (60km/37mi northeast of Almería). *Daily | book 1–2 days in advance | admission from 13 euros | tel. 9 50 36 47 04 | www.cuevasdesorbas.com*

MOJÁCAR ☼ (147 F4) (ⓜ O5)

Many of the white buildings on the hillside in Mojácar (pop. 8000, 93km/58mi northeast of Almería), which enjoy far-reaching views over the Mediterranean,

have been there since the days of the Moors. Down on the coast, 2km (1¼mi) from the old village, hotels, bars and restaurants all vie for space, although it is not as cramped as on the Costa del Sol. A 7km (4½mi)-long sandy beach is on the doorstep. One lovely little hotel in the old part with a view of the sea is *Mamabel's (8 rooms | C/Embajadores 5 | tel. 9 50 47 24 48 | www.mamabels.com | Budget)*; room no. 1 is ideal for romantics; good restaurant. You can stay in more elegant accommodation right on the beach in the recently renovated *Parador (98 rooms | Playa de Mojácar | tel. 9 50 47 82 50 | www.parador.es | Expensive)*. Information: *Oficina de Turismo (Plaza del Frontón | tel. 9 02 57 51 30 | www.mojacar.es)*

MARCO POLO HIGHLIGHTS

★ **Parque Natural Cabo de Gata**
Rugged scenery and wonderful, idyllic beaches → **p. 62**

★ **Cazorla**
A little town surrounded by a huge Natural Park → **p. 63**

★ **Albaicín**
Granada's labyrinthine Moorish Quarter → **p. 65**

★ **Alhambra**
The magnificent palace complex in Granada → **p. 67**

★ **Alpujarras**
Whitewashed villages dotted about the Sierra Nevada → **p. 72**

★ **Baeza and Úbeda**
The most beautiful Renaissance towns in the country → **p. 74**

Wildly romantic rocky coastline at Cabo de Gata east of Almería

PARQUE NATURAL CABO DE GATA ★
(147 E–F 5–6) (*ℳ N–06*)

South of San José (40km/25mi northeast of Almería) a track leads to what are perhaps the most beautiful beaches on Andalucía's Mediterranean coastline. A migrating dune amidst this volcanic landscape separates the wide, crescent-shaped *Playa de los Genoveses* and the hidden beach *Cala Los Amarillos* where you can bathe in the nude without being disturbed. The adjoining ● *Playa del Mónsul* and the 'Crescent Beach', *Medialuna*, are surrounded by unique rock formations. Cortijo del Fraile, the scene of a drama that Federlco García Lorca focused on in his play Blood Wedding, is beyond the abandoned gold mines of Rodalquilar. Fresh fish and paella with a wonderful view of the bay can be enjoyed in the ⚘ *Restaurante Isleta del Moro (right on the harbourside | tel. 9 50 38 97 13 | Budget–*

Moderate) in the dreamy little fishing village of *Isleta del Moro*. Sophisticated Mediterranean cuisine is served in the delightful *La Gallineta (Pozo de Los Frailes | tel. 9 50 38 05 01 | Moderate–Expensive)*. The **INSIDER TIP** *Cala del Plomo*, a secluded bay perfect for swimming, is reached from picturesque Agua Amarga in about 40 mins. along a lovely path.

One of the best places to stay in the park is the ecologically-run Casa Rural ☺ *La Joya de Cabo de Gata (Paraje La Joya, Agua Amarga | tel. 6 19 15 95 87 | www.lajoyadecabodegata.es | Moderate–Expensive)*. Apart from two charming ⚘ apartments (sleeping up to 4) with terraces and a wonderful view, a cosy but spacious **INSIDER TIP** Bedouin tent is also available.

Information: *Oficina de Turismo in San José (Avda. San José 27 | tel. 9 50 38 02 99); Visitor centre for Las Almoladeras Nature*

CAZORLA

Park (Ctra. Cabo de Gata–Almería | tel. 9 50 16 04 35 | www.parquenatural.com | www.cabodegata.net)

WESTERN SETS IN THE TABERNAS DESERT (147 D4–5) (*⌀ N5*)

A number of epic 'spaghetti westerns', such as *Once Upon a Time in the West*, were filmed in the 1960s in the desert regions inland from Almería. When there is no filming, three 'towns' used as sets entertain visitors to a western spectacle: *Parque Temático Oasys Mini Hollywood (N340a, at km 464 | daily 10am–9pm, in winter 7pm | admission 20 euros | (www.oasysparque tematico.com)* with western town, open-air swimming pool, zoo and leisure park; *Texas Hollywood (N340a, at km 468 | daily 9am–8pm, in winter 6pm | admission 17 euros | www.fortbravo.es)* and *Western Leone (A92, at km 378 | daily 10am–8pm, in winter 6pm | admission 12 euros)*.

(141 E3) (*⌀ L3*) ★ The infrastructure of this pretty mountain town is ideal for tours of Spain's largest Natural Park – the Parque Natural Cazorla, Segura y Las Villas.

Cazorla (pop. 9000), in the east of Jaén province, is located in the heart of the countryside. The Sierra de Cazorla, with the little town of Cazorla on its edge, is the second largest protected area in Europe. Pine and holm oak forests cover great swathes of the countryside that covers 826mi², intersected by rivers and reservoirs, with Alpine mountains and barren steppes. The A 319 leads you over the 1290m (4232ft)-high Puerto de las Palomas into the park.

Go for a walk along the Cerrada de Utrero to the first reservoir built on the Guadalquivir or take a several hour-long hike along the Río Borosa to the Laguna de Valdeazores. Alternatively visit the source of the Guadalquivir that is not far from Cazorla itself. Drivers can follow the *Ruta Félix Rodríguez de la Fuente* around the Embalse (reservoir) del Tranco and art lovers will enjoy the museum with works by the Expressionist Rafael Zabaleta in Quesada.

SIGHTSEEING

Cars are best left in the multi-storey car park under the Plaza Mercado from where you can explore the narrow and picturesque mountain town on foot. A steep path leads up from the pretty *Plaza de Santa María* with its ruined church of the same name to the sturdy *Castillo de la Yedra* and a folk art museum which is well worth a visit *(Tue 3pm–8pm, Wed–Sat 9am–8pm, Sun 9am–2pm | admission free)*.

FOOD & DRINK

MESÓN LEANDRO
Barbecued meat is a speciality of this rustic restaurant. *Daily | C/La Hoz 3 | tel. 9 53 72 06 32 | Budget–Moderate*

LA SARGA
The best restaurant here, located below the Old Town, offers innovative regional fare. *Closed Tue | Plaza del Mercado s/n | tel. 9 53 72 15 07 | Moderate*

SPORTS & ACTVITIES

Riding, hiking, cycling, trekking through the Sierra or kayaking on the El Tranco reservoir are just a few of many possible activities offered by local companies such as *www.tierraventuracazorla.com*, *www.turisnat.es* or *www.cazorlaextremenature.com*.

Further details available at the tourist information office.

WHERE TO STAY

INSIDER TIP MOLINO LA FARRAGA
Something very special near the Old Town, yet in the countryside – a watermill converted into a guesthouse. *8 rooms | Camino de la Hoz | tel. 9 53 72 12 49 | www.molinolafarraga.com | Budget–Moderate*

PARADOR
Wonderful location in the Natural Park. Its particular charm lies in its slightly old-fashioned atmosphere. Breathtaking mountain panorama from the pool. 24km (15mi) from Cazorla. *36 rooms | tel. 9 53 72 70 75 | Moderate–Expensive*

SIERRA DE CAZORLA & SPA ☺
The hotel is on the mountain road above La Iruela. The large spa area with outdoor and indoor pools is heated using biomass fuel (such as olive stones). *40 rooms | Ctra. de la Sierra s/n | La Iruela | tel. 9 53 72 00 15 | www.hotelsierradecazorla.com | Moderate*

INFORMATION

OFICINAS DE TURISMO
Plaza de Santa María | tel. 9 53 71 01 02 | www.cazorla.es, www.turismoencazorla.com. Centro Interpretación de la Torre del Vinagre (Ctra. del Tranco | A-319 km 48,8)

GRANADA

▨ MAP INSIDE BACK COVER
(145 E3) (*🛿 K5*) Saturday evening on the *Carrera del Darro*. Night owls take over the street, language school pupils, students, young Spaniards and masses of foreigners gather here, drifting from bar to bar, laughing, chatting, casually or intimately arm in arm.

Tourists mingle in the crowd and let themselves be carried along by the happy jostling, caught in the magic of night-time Granada. The Alhambra up above seems to hover over the scene, bathed in soft floodlighting. Opposite the fortress, the labyrinthine streets of the Albaicín, the old Moorish Quarter, are silent.

CITY WHERE TO START?
Plaza Nueva: Head for the Plaza Nueva. From here it is just a short distance to the cathedral, Capilla Real and the narrow streets of the Albaicín district. The car park in Calle del Cristo de San Agustín, near Gran Vía is very central. Or follow the car park routing system. Bus no. 33 starts at the station with several stops along the Gran Vía.

Always full of people – a café in the Albaicín, Granada's Moorish Old Town

Granada (pop. 240,000) is a lively university city and, at the same time, the keeper of a precious past. In the course of the 13th century, when large parts of Spain fell into the hands of the Christians, Muhammad I of the Nasrid dynasty, made a pact with the Catholics that enabled him to found a Muslim kingdom in Granada. Over the following 250 years, Granada remained an island of civilisation during the Dark Ages. Proof of the Nasrids' cultural superiority is their royal palace, the Alhambra, which was built on the orders of Muhammad I in 1238. Ultimately, the Christians' urge to conquer was greater than any refined lifestyle and so, on 2 January, 1492, Spain's last Muslim ruler, Boabdil (Muhammad XII), handed over the keys of the city to the Catholic Queen Isabella of Castile and Ferdinand of Aragón. The Alhambra is one of the most beautiful palaces in the world and an exceptional testimony to Islamic rule in Andalucía. More than 2 million visitors come here every year to marvel as this World Heritage Site. Anyone approaching the city from the west will automatically be captivated by its magical setting. Granada lies at an altitude of 685m (2250ft) below the peaks of the Sierra Nevada which remain snow-covered well into spring. Passing through the badly planned suburbs may dampen your enthusiasm a little, but this evil is one Granada shares with all major cities in Spain. (For more detailed information see the MARCO POLO guidebook 'Costa del Sol').

SIGHTSEEING

ALBAICÍN ★

The hill opposite the Alhambra, now the district of Albaicín, was the first area in present-day Granada to be settled – from the 7th century onwards – by the Iberians, Romans and Visigoths. However, it was not until the 11th century, under Arabian rule, that it became important. The district still retains its Moorish character even though none of the present buildings actually date from that time, apart from the ruins of the town wall and the gateways. Following the expulsion of the Mosiscos (Muslims forced to convert to Christianity) at the end of the 16th century, many of the buildings fell into disrepair. Bigger properties with walled gardens, called *carmen* – for which Albaicín is famous today – were constructed on the sites. *Carmen Max Moreau (Camino nuevo de San Nicolás 12 | Tue–Sat 10am–1.30pm, 4pm–6pm)* and *Carmen Aljibe del Rey (guided tours Tue–Fri 12 noon)* are open to visitors. For those who like exploring, just wander around the narrow streets seeing where a stairway may lead to, winding your way between white-washed buildings without any particular destination in mind. Muslim traditions and culture have now been revived here and, in 2004, the first modern-day mosque in Andalucía, the *Mezquita Mayor*, was opened. Its gardens are open to the public. The liveliest squares are the *Placeta de San Miguel Bajo* and the shady *Plaza Larga*. From the ● ⚜ *Mirador San Nicolás* you can enjoy an unsurpassed view of the Alhambra. The *Palacio de Dar al-Horra (Callejón de las Monjas | Tue/Thu/Sat 10am–2pm)* where Boabdil's mother is reputed to have lived, and the Arabian baths *El Bañuelo (Tue/Thu 2.30pm–8.00pm, Wed/Fri/Sat 9am–8pm, Sun 9am–2pm | admission free | Carrera del Darro 34)*, that date from the 11th century, are also well worth a visit. To the west is the 'Holy Mountain', *Sacromonte* where ruins of the old town wall can be found

The majestic Alhambra in the evening light against the backdrop of the Sierra Nevada

as well as several cave dwellings. This is the traditional district of Granada where the *gitanos* (the Romani people) live. The former Jewish Quarter, ✂ *Realejo*, on the southern slope of the Alhambra, is an inviting place for a walk and is slowly being discovered by outsiders. Or else you can head for one of the bars on the lively Campo del Príncipe.

ALHAMBRA ⭐

The interior of the Alhambra ('the Red One') is like a treasure trove hidden behind mighty walls void of any ornamentation. These enclose a site divided into several totally different parts. At the western-most end are the remains of the Alcazaba, the citadel and administrative section. The ✂ *Torre de la Vela* boasts views in two directions – to the north to Albaicín and to the south to the Sierra Nevada. The heart

of the Alhambra however is formed by the *Palacios Nazaríes* (the Nasrid Palaces). Having passed the entrance, you begin to get an impression of the magnificence to come in the *Mexuar* (audience and council chamber) and the *Cuarto Dorado* (Golden Room). The first highlight of any visit to the palace is the adjoining *Patio de los Arrayanes* (Court of the Myrtles) and the *Sala de los Embajadores* (Hall of the Ambassadors) next door. The throne used by the Nasrid kings was most probably placed under the wonderful *artesonado* inlaid ceiling made of thousands of small cedar tiles. This leads on to the *Patio de los Leones* (Court of the Lions), the most popular photographic motif in the Alhambra. Twelve stone lions are in the middle of the courtyard, bottom to bottom, under a marble basin. The *Sala de los Abencerrajes* (Hall of the Abencerrages) casts a magic of its own. The dome looks like a plaster sea of dripping honeycomb which has solidified and turned white and is reflected in the twelve-sided basin in the floor. You leave the Nasrid magic behind you on entering the *Palace of Charles V (mid Oct–mid March 9am–6pm, mid March–May and Sept 10am–8pm, June–mid Sept 9am–3.30pm on Tue–Sat, Sun all year round 10am–5pm | admission 1.50 euros)* that the emperor ordered to be built inside the Alhambra. Construction work on this severe Renaissance building started in 1526. Externally square and internally round, it now houses the Museum of Fine Arts. Works from the 15th–20th centuries are displayed in nine rooms. Paintings by Alonso Cano are among the most important works. The *Parador* – which is continuously fully booked – is also located within the walls of the Alhambra. The bar is a cool oasis of peace and quiet. A visit to the ✂ blossoming gardens around the summer palace, the *Generalife*, beyond the Alhambra is not to be left out.

Avoid having to get up early, queueing for hours and the frustration of not being able to visit the Alhambra because of the restricted number of visitors (6600 a day) by buying your entrance ticket online under *www.alhambra-tickets.es* or by phone *(8am–midnight) tel. 9 02 88 80 01* in Spain or, from abroad, *tel. 34 9 34 92 37 50* (with a credit card). You may also be able to buy tickets in your hotel. In Spain, you can also book through branches of the Caixa Bank. Same-day tickets are available at the cashdesk at the entrance to the Alhambra – but only when that day's quota has not been exhausted – or at the *Tienda Librería de la Alhambra, C/Reyes Católicos 40*. Admission to the Palacios Nazaríes is only possible at the time printed on the tickets; morning visitors must leave the Alhambra by 2pm. As the *Bono Turístico (concessions and vouchers valid for 5 days | 32.50 euros)* has its own allotment of tickets, it may well be worth buying such a ticket. *March–Oct daily 8.30am–8pm, late evening visits (Palacios Nazaríes) Tue–Sat 10pm–11.30pm, Nov–Feb daily 8.30am–6pm, evening visits Fri/Sat 8pm–9.30pm | admission 13 euros | www.alhambra-patronato.es*

CATEDRAL AND LOWER CITY AREA

Completely surrounded by other buildings, the cathedral *Santa María de la Encarnación (Mon–Sat 10am–1.30pm, 4pm–8pm, Sun 4pm–8pm | admission 4 euros)* has little room to impress visitors with its exterior. This is more than made up for inside. This, the first Renaissance cathedral in Spain, is largely the work fo the architect Diego de Siloé. The round *Capilla Mayor,* 22m (72ft) in diameter, 45m (148ft) high, is striking. Right next to the cathedral is the Royal Chapel, the *Capilla Real (Mon–Sat 10.15am–1.30pm, Sun 11am–1pm and daily 4pm–7.30pm | admission 4 euros | C/Oficios 3)* which, since 1521, is where the Catholic monarchs Isabella of Castile and Ferdinand of Aragón are buried. Next to them is the tomb of their daughter Joanna the Mad and her husband Philip the Handsome. Isabella's personal

FEDERICO GARCÍA LORCA

Federico García Lorca (1898–1936) is considered Spain's greatest poet and dramatist of the early 20th century. He became friends with Dalí and Luis Buñuel while still a student in Madrid. He always remained close to his homeland, Andalucía, as recorded in works such as *Blood Wedding* and *Romanceros Gitanos*, his 'Gypsy Ballads'. He lived ansd worked in his country house *Huerta de San Vicente* on the outskirts of Granada from 1925 until his assassination by Falangists in 1936 *(mid June–mid Sept Tue–Sun 9.15am–2.15pm, April, May, beginning of June/end of Sept also 5pm–8pm, Oct–March also 4pm–7pm | guided tours daily except Mon | admission incl. guided tour 3 euros | C/Virgen Blanca s/n | www.huertadesanvicente. com).* The poet was born in Fuente Vaqueros (18km/11mi west of Granada). The house and museum are also open to the public *(closed Mon, guided tours Tue–Sat mornings | admission 1.80 euros | www.museogarcialorca.org).* Lorca also mirrored his experience in *Yerma* and *The House of Bernarda Alba*. It is believed that Lorca is buried on the edge of Alfacar (8km/5mi northeast of Granada). *www.turgranada.es*

INSIDER TIP *collection of paintings from the 15th century*, including masterpieces by van der Weyden and Botticelli, hang in an adjoining room. To the south are the narrow streets of the *Alcaicería* area. This was where silk and cloth sellers had their shops during the Moorish era; today you can find everything that the souvenir industry has to offer. At the heart of the bustling city centre is the *Plaza Bib-Rambla* with its many cafés. Cardinal Cisneros, Isabella's Father Confessor, masterminded the burning of books here in 1499 during which the majority of Arabian writings in Al-Andalus were lost. The *Corral de Carbón (Carrera Mariana Pineda)* is the oldest Arabian structure in Granada. The former 'caravanserai' (trading inn) was later used as a theatre and coal store – which gave it its present name.

MONASTERIO DE LA CARTUJA

The building of this Charterhouse monastery was started in 1514 and not completed until 1794. It is an exceptional example of the exuberant Spanish Baroque style. *Daily 10am–1pm, 4pm–8pm, Nov–March 3pm–6pm | admission 4 euros | Paseo de la Cartuja | north of the city centre*

The Plaza Bib-Rambla in the centre of Granada

FOOD & DRINK

BODEGAS CASTAÑEDA

A bar straight out of a picture-book – old wine barrels, a wooden drinks bar, a bull's head and delicious tapas. *Daily | C/Almireceros 1 | tel. 9 58 22 32 22 | Budget*

LOS DIAMANTES

Neon lighting and no hip design elements, yet there are few tapas bars in Granada that have as much atmosphere as here. Good, generous helpings. Other tapas bars can be found in the Calle Navas. *Closed Sun | C/ Navas 26 | Budget*

MIRADOR DE MORAYMA ☺ ☘

In a former *palacio* in Albaicín. Beautiful interior with antique furnishings. Wonderful view of the Alhambra from the terrace. Organic wine from its own vineyards. *Closed Sun evening | Pianista García Carrillo 2 | tel. 9 58 22 82 90 | Moderate–Expensive*

INSIDER TIP TABERNA LA TANA

Small as this tapas bar may be, the choice of excellent wines is huge and the little snacks a real treat. *Daily | C/Rosario s/n | Budget–Moderate*

LAS TINAJAS

The locals swear by this traditional place a little off the beaten track. Cosy atmosphere and delicious tapas in the bar. *Daily | C/Martínez Campos 17 | tel. 9 58 25 43 93 | Moderate–Expensive*

The Moorish fortress Almuñécar

SHOPPING

In the Alcaicería between the cathedral and the Plaza Bib-Rambla, are the buildings of the Alcaicería itself – the old market – which now specialise in jewellery and crafted items for the tourist trade, hemmed in by other souvenir shops. The approach to the Alhambra in the *Cuesta de Gomérez* presents a similar picture. A bazaar-like atmosphere can be found in the streets Calderería Nueva and Vieja at the foot of the Albaicín with tea rooms, restaurants and lots of shops. Hand-made ceramics *(e.g. Cerámicas Fajalauza (C/ Fajalauza 2)*, marquetry and guitar making *(Miguel Ángel Bellido (C/Navas 22)* and *Daniel Gil de Avalle (Plaza del Realejo 15)* have a long tradition in Granada. Local culinary specialities as well as Andalucían olive oil can be found, for example, in *La Oliva* at Calle Rosario 9.

ENTERTAINMENT

At weekends there is always a lot going on around the *Plaza Nueva* and in the *Calle Elvira* and *Carrera del Darro* where there are several tapas and cocktail bars and the disco *Granada 10 (C/Cárcel Baja 10)*. The disco and club *Camborio* is on the road to the *gitano* district Sacromonte. The best-known and largest nightclub is *Mae West (in the Neptuno shopping centre | C/Pedro Antonio de Alarcón)*, south of the city centre.

FLAMENCO

The flamenco is performed in the caves of Sacromonte beyond the Albaicín. The price includes the show, being picked up from your hotel and a guided tour of the Albaicín. Recommended performances: *Cueva La Rocío (daily 10pm | admission 25 euros | Camino del Sacromonte 70 | tel. 9 58 22 71 29); Venta El Gallo (daily from 7.30pm | admission 22 euros | Barranco de los Negros 5 | tel. 9 58 22 24 92 | www. ventaelgallo.com)*.

WHERE TO STAY

HOTEL ABADES NEVADA PALACE

This new business and designer hotel is situated between the city centre (easily reached by bus) and the city expressway. Trips to the surrounding countryside from here are easy. Spa and outdoor pool. Advance reservation advisable. *235 rooms, 23 apartments | C/de la Sultana 3 | tel. 9 02 22 25 70 | www.abadesnevadapalace.com | Budget–Expensive*

BRITZ

This simple but cheap guesthouse is not exactly quietly but centrally located on the Plaza Nueva. The rooms are clean and the service friendly and informal. *22 rooms | Cuesta de Gomérez 1 | tel. 9 58 22 36 52 | www.pensionbritz.com | Budget*

CASA 1800

Until recently Los Migueletes city palace at the foot of the Albaicín was a designer hotel. Now it exudes a neo-Baroque opulence with exquisite materials and good service. *25 rooms | Benalúa 11 | tel. 9 58 21 07 00 | www.hotelcasa1800granada.com | Expensive*

INSIDER TIP ▶ GAR ANAT HOTEL PEREGRINOS

Mika Murakami has transformd the interior of this historical town palace into a poetic stage. Those who like such things will be full of enthusiasm for this new hotel. *Placeta de los Peregrinos 1 | tel. 9 58 22 55 28 | www.hoteldeperegrinos.com | Moderate–Expensive*

MACÍA PLAZA

The uncomplicated and practical location on the Plaza Nueva has always been a plus point of this 2-star hotel. The rooms have been modernised in keeping with the times. *44 rooms | Plaza Nueva 5 | tel. 9 58 22 75 36 | www.maciahoteles.com | Moderate*

AC PALACIO DE SANTA PAULA

This luxury hotel near the cathedral combines the magnificence of the 19th century with contemporary design. *75 rooms | Gran Vía de Colón 31 | tel. 9 58 80 57 40 |* www.ac-hotels.com *| Expensive*

INFORMATION

OFICINA DE TURISMO

Plaza Marian Pineda 10; C/Santa Ana 4 (right next to the Plaza Nueva). Plaza del Carmen | tel. 9 02 40 50 45; other information offices in the Alhambra and on the Plaza Bib-Rambla. *www.turismodegranada.org, www.granada.org, www.granadatur.com*

WHERE TO GO

ALMUÑÉCAR (145 E5) (*∅ K6*)

A popular seaside resort (pop. 28,000, 78km/49mi south of Granada) on the Costa Tropical (the Mediterranean coast in Granada province). The long, clean pebbly beaches have been rather spoilt by new buildings but the Old Town is lovely for a

LOW BUDGET

▶ With the tourist card *Bono Turístico Granada* you can use the tourist bus service and save 30% on entrance fees. What is probably more important is that you can visit the Alhambra on the ticket when it is otherwise often difficult obtaining tickets through normal channels due to allocation restrictions. 25–31 euros; further information under *www.granatur.com*

▶ Buy the delicious, healthy, extra native local olive oil directly from the producer, e.g. the excellent organic oil 'Verde Salud' from the Sierra Mágina. *Trujal de Mágina, Llanos de Ochoa | Cambil (Jaén) | www.scatrujaldemagina.com*

stroll. The Moorish fortress *Castillo San Miguel (Tue–Sat 10.30am–1.30pm, 5pm– 7.30pm, Sun 10.30–2pm | admission 2.40 euros)* is situated above the town. The Archaeological Museum with Roman and Phoenician finds is close by. The largest sea aquarium in Andalucía, ● *Acuario Almuñécar (depending on the season either daily 10.30am–10pm or 10am–6.30pm | admission 12 euros | Plaza Kuwait | www. acuarioalmunecar.es)*, is home to some 3000 marine animals. The seahorses are the highlight. Head for the Calle Manila in the centre for a bite to eat. There are several tapas bars here such as the popular *La Bodeguita*. Almuñécar's most beautiful hotel is the *Casablanca (35 rooms | Plaza San Cristóbal 4 | tel. 9 58 63 55 75 | www. hotelcasablancaalmunecar.com | Budget)*. Information: *Oficina de Turismo im Palacete de la Najarra (Avda. de Europa | tel. 9 58 63 11 25 | www.almunecar.info)*

ALPUJARRAS ★ (145 F4) *(∅ K6)*

Dozens of little villages from the Moorish period lie hidden in the fantastic barren mountains on the southern side of the Sierra Nevada. Settlers brought their know-how from the Atlas Mountains in Morocco with them, cut terraces, planted and irrigated fields and left a form of architecture unique in Andalucía. The flat slate roofs are covered with *launa*, a black soil that absorbs rainwater.

An excursion to ☀ *Poqueira Valley (Valle de Poqueira)* (67km/42mi from Granada) and its three villages Pampaneira, Bubión and *Capileira* is well worthwhile. The cosy Arabian-Andalucían restaurant *Ibero (closed Sun evening and Mon | C/Parra 1 | tel. 6 53 93 50 56 | Budget–Moderate)* is in Capileira. The lovely hotel *Finca los Llanos (40 rooms | Ctra. de Sierra Nevada | tel. 9 58 76 30 71 | www.hotelfincalosllanos. com | Budget)* is situated on the outskirts. Information (in Pampaneira): *Centro de*

Visitantes (Plaza Libertad | tel. 9 58 76 31 27 | www.nevadensis.com). Trevélez (1480m/ 4856ft), 25km (15½mi) further east, calls itself the 'highest settlment in Spain', which is not actually true. The locals are also convinced that their ham is the best in Spain. Whatever the case, Trevélez is still very pretty, even without this distinction, and its ham is delicious indeed.

GUADIX (145 F3) *(∅ L5)*

Whitewashed chimneys peek out of the brown earth and the fronts of houses cling to rock faces – there are some 1300 cave dwellings scattered around the district of Santiago in Guadix (pop. 20,000, 58km/36m east of Granada). Even in pre-Roman times people dug into the earth here; today, the caves are comfortably equipped. Follow signs to the Barriada de Cuevas. The Moorish *Alcazaba* and the 15th-century cathedral are also noteworthy. The Renaissance building was designed by Diego de Siloé who is also immortal-

ised by the cathedral in Granada. For a place to eat and stay the night try the well-run *Comercio (42 rooms | C/Mira de Amezcua 3 | tel. 9 58 66 05 00 | www.hotel comercio.com | Budget–Moderate)*. Set against the frequently snow-covered peaks of the Sierra Nevada is the Renaissance castle of La Calahorra with its four round towers, 15km (9½mi) further to the east *(Wed 10am–1pm, 4pm–6pm)*. Information: *Oficina de Turismo (Avda. Mariana Pineda s/n | tel. 9 58 69 95 74 | www.guadixymar quesado.org)*.

SALOBREÑA (145 E5) (ℳ K6)

This white village (pop. 13,000, 62km/ 39mi south of Granada) lies on a rocky prominence on the Costa Tropical. Steep, narrow streets wind their way up the mountain between houses covered with flowers to a ❀ Moorish *Castillo* (13th century) at the top. The village is surrounded by sugarcane plantations. However, the plain that stretches as far as the beach,

is losing its charm with every new hotel and apartment block. *Pesetas (closed Mon | C/Bóveda 11 | tel. 9 58 61 01 82 | Budget)* specialises in grilled fish. It is up in the Old Town and boasts a lovely roof terrace. *Hostal Jayma (13 rooms | C/Cristo 24 | tel. 9 58 61 02 31 | www.hostaljayma.com | Budget)* is a well maintained hostel just below the Old Town. Information: *Oficina de Turismo (Plaza Goya s/n | tel. 9 58 61 03 13 | www.ayto-salobrena.org)*

SIERRA NEVADA (145 E–F4) (ℳ K5)

The highest mountains on the Spanish mainland are *Mulhacén* (3481m/11,420ft) and *Pico de Veleta* (3398m/11,148ft) in the 'Snowy Range' near Granada. This is not only where Europe's most southerly skiing area is to be found but also Spain's largest national park. And these 332mi² are in turn surrounded by an area listed as a Natural Park, home to the ibex and eagle. Depending on the season and your mood there is a wide-range of things to

Fantastic view of the rocky outcrop and the Bay of Salobreña

do – albeit outside the protected areas – from skiing or mountain biking, hiking, riding or climbing, to tours in off-road vehicles. Further details and maps available from the information centre in the national park: *Centro de Visitantes El Donajo (April–Sept daily 10am–2pm, 6pm–8pm, Oct–March daily 10am–2pm, 4pm–6pm | A395 to Pradollano, at km 23 | tel. 9 58 34 06 25 | www.sierranevada.es | www.nevadensis.com)*

JAÉN

(140 B4) *(𝄢 J3)* The provincial capital (pop. 117,000), located on a hill with the Sierra de la Pandera rising up behind, forms a gateway to Andalucía.

The *Renaissance cathedral (Mon–Sat 8.30am–1pm, 5pm–8pm, Sun 9am–1.30pm, 6pm–8pm | admission 5 euros)* towers above the labyrinthine narrow streets of the markedly Arabian Old Town. The vaulted Arabian baths from the 11th century are beneath the *Palacio Villardompardo* which itself houses a folk museum *(Tue–Sat 9am–8.15pm, Sun 9am–3pm, in winter Tue–Fri 9am–8pm, Sat–Sun 9.30am–2.30pm | admission free)*. The best collection of Iberian art in

Spain is in the ● *Museo de Jaén (Tue 2.30pm–8.30pm, Wed–Sat 9am–8.30pm, Sun 9am–2.30pm | free admission for EU citizens | Paseo de la Estación 29)*. The sculptures of fascinating real and mythological creatures have their very own tales to tell. The ☇ *Castillo de Santa Catalina*, originally built by the Moors, towers above the town and offers a view over what has made Jaén so famous – its olive groves with row upon row of trees.

FOOD & DRINK

The Plaza del Posito is a pleasant square with bars and cafés. Tapas bars such as rustic *La Manchega (C/Bernardo López 8)* can be found on and around the *Calle Cerón.*

CASA ANTONIO

The best restaurant in town. Superb quality classic and creative *cocina alta. Closed Sun evening | C/Fermín Palma 3 | tel. 9 53 27 02 62 | Expensive*

WHERE TO STAY

PARADOR DE JAÉN

The Castillo de Santa Catalina is now a beautiful Parador. The restaurant in the Great Hall is also to be recommended. *45 rooms | Castillo de Santa Catalina | tel. 9 53 23 00 00 | www.parador.es | Expensive*

INFORMATION

Oficina de Turismo
C/Ramón y Cajal 4 | tel. 9 53 31 32 81 | www. turjaen.org, www. promojaen.es

WHERE TO GO

BAEZA AND ÚBEDA ★
46km (29mi) and 54km (33½mi) northeast of Jaén and about 8km (5mi) apart

🏙 WHERE TO START?

Plaza de la Constitución: The upper part of Jaén around the cathedral is fascinating. From here you can explore the Old Town and the Palacio de Villardompardo. The local museum is a 10-min. walk from here. The underground car park near the Plaza de la Constitución is convenient. Bus routes 1 and 2 link the museum, among other places, with the Plaza de la Constitución.

are Spain's two most beautiful Renaissance towns that have both been declared Unesco World Heritage Sites.

In *Baeza* (140 C3) (*ω K3*), with a population of 16,000, visitors find themselves in a world of its own around the two squares Santa Cruz and Santa María. The *Palacio Jabalquinto* (15th–17th centuries) is embellished with a façade in the Isabelline Gothic style. The plain Late Romanesque church of *Santa Cruz* diagonally opposite provides a stark contrast. The *Antigua Universidad* opened its doors in 1542. The *Plaza de Santa María* with the 16th-century cathedral, the *Seminario de San Felipe Neri* (now the International University) and the *Casas Consistoriales* is a picturesque ensemble. A similarly harmonious picture can be found on the *Plaza del Pópulo* with the Roman lion sculptures of the *Fuente de Leones*. A former abattoir *(Antigua Carnicería)* fronts the square. Its façade is just as magnificently decorated as that of the Casa del Pópulo. You can eat well at Vandelvira *(closed Sun/Mon | C/San Francisco 14 | tel. 9 53 74 81 72 | Moderate)* where the head chef, María Salomé Delgado, conjures up regional delicacies in a former Renaissance monastery. The best olive oil in the area can be found at the INSIDER TIP *Casa de Aceite (Paseo de la Constitución 9). The Hospedería Fuentenueva (13 rooms | C/Carmen 15 | tel. 9 53 74 31 00 | www.fuentenueva.com | Budget)* is one possible place to spend the night. The former woman's prison is now a colourful hotel. Information: *Plaza del Pópulo | tel. 9 53 74 04 44 | www.baeza.net*. In *Úbeda* (141 D3) (*ω K3*), (pop. 36,000), follow signs to the Parador and you will reach the *Plaza Vázquez de Molina*, surrounded by magnificent 16th-century architecture in all its glory – the *Palacio de las Cadenas*, the church *Santa María de los Reales Alcázares*, the granary *Antiguo Pósito*, the *Capilla del Salvador* and the

nobles' palace *Deán Ortega* which is now a Parador *(tel. 9 53 75 03 45 | www.parador. es | Moderate–Expensive)*. If you plan on staying here, ask for INSIDER TIP room no. 112 – the corner room opposite the main entrance to the *Capilla del Salvador*. Passing the *Capilla del Salvador* with its Renaissance façade by Andrés de

Richly decorated façade of the Palacio de Jabalquinto in Baeza

Vandelvira and the Hospital del Salvador, is the ● ⚓ *Plaza Santa Lucía*, from where there are far-reaching views over endless olive groves. The church *Santa María* with its cloisters, the *town hall* and *San Pablo* are all well worth visiting, as is the inner courtyard of the *Hospital de Santiago*. Beautiful ceramic items are for sale at the INSIDER TIP *Alfarería Tito pottery studio (Plaza del Ayuntamiento 12)*. The workshop museum *Paco Tito (C/Valencia 12)* is interesting. Good home cooking can be enjoyed at *El Seco (Sun–Thu afternoons only | Corazón de Jesús 8 | tel. 9 53 79 14 52 | Moderate)*. Information: *C/Baja del marqués 4 | tel. 9 53 75 08 97 | www. promojaen.es*

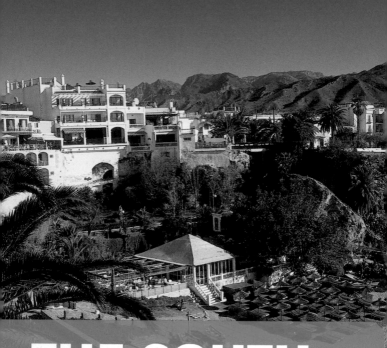

THE SOUTH

The sun, sand and sea attract millions of visitors every year from all over the world to the beaches on the Costa del Sol (for more detailed information see the MARCO POLO guidebook 'Costa del Sol') and the Costa de la Luz between Nerja and Sanlúcar de Barrameda.

The real attraction of the Andalucían south, however, which covers the provinces of Cádiz and Málaga, lies inland from the rows of huge tourist hotels. The enchanting 'White Towns' in the Sierra de Grazalema epitomise the dream of the Moorish south. Only romantic Ronda on the split rocky plateau can hold its own in the face of such untamed beauty. The addition 'de la

Frontera' to many names is a reminder of the Reconquista period when the Christians regained control and when the borders between Catholic and Moorish Spain were constantly changing in the hard fought-over south. During this era under the rule of the Almohad dynasty enormous fortress complexes, Arabian baths and small mosques were built.

CÁDIZ

(142 A4) (*∭ C7*) Everyone in ⭐ Cádiz (pop. 125,000) can be found on the Campo del Sur or the Alameda de

Photo: The rocky coastline at Nerja on the Costa del Sol

Escape from the concrete jungle to one of the many beautiful beaches and explore the magical white villages further inland

Apodaca early in the evening, out to enjoy the sea air and soak in the last rays of sun as it sets over the sea.

Europe's oldest city (founded in the 11th century BC by the Phoenicians) is flanked by the Atlantic on three sides and defended by a circular wall facing the sea. Only in the west is there a small beach. Within the city wall Baroque townhouses, some with tall lookout towers, dominate the

CITY WHERE TO START?
Start at the **Plaza San Juan de Díos** near the Town Hall where there are also several places to park. From here it is not far to the cathedral. Coaches and ferries from Puerto de Santa María will bring to you the outskirts of the Old Town.

CÁDIZ

The huge cathedral dominates the silhouette of the Old Town in Cádiz

scene. It was from here that the merchants would keep watch to see when their ships were approaching the harbour. In 1717 Cádiz was granted a monopoly for trading with Latin America which had previously brought considerable wealth to Sevilla. This charming city of the *Gaditanos*, as the people of Cádiz are called, is characterised by its mass of little squares.

SIGHTSEEING

CASTILLO DE SANTA CATALINA 🔅
16th-century fortress with star-shaped floor plan on the city's west bank *(daily 10am–7.45pm, in summer 8.45pm | admission free)*. To the north is the small, romantic *Parque Genovés*.

CATEDRAL
The cathedral made of sandstone, jasper and marble (1722–1838, with Baroque and neo-Classical elements) gleams in the sun. One of Spain's most important 20th-century composers, Manuel de Falla (1876–1946), was born in Cádiz and is buried in the crypt. The entry fee to the cathedral includes the *Museo de la Catedral (Mon–Sat 10am–6.30pm, Sun 1.30pm–6.30pm | admission 5 euros)* in the Casa de Contaduría on the Plaza Fray Félix. The 🔅 *Torre de Poniente* (west tower) offers a magnificent view over the city. *Guided tours every 30 mins. | admission 5 euros*

HOSPITAL DE MUJERES
Two lovely green inner courtyards lie hidden inside the Baroque former women's hospital. The painting *The Ecstasy of St Francis* by El Greco hangs in a side chapel. *Mon–Fri 8am–2pm, 5.30pm–8.30pm, Sat 10am–1.30pm | admission free | C/Hospital de Mujeres 26*

MUSEO DE CÁDIZ ●
Archaeology and art in one building. Treasures include two sarcophaguses from the Phoenician period (5th century BC), a statue of Emperor Trajan found in the Roman settlement and artworks from the 16th–20th centuries. **INSIDER TIP** The collection of paintings by Zurbarán is unique.

The exceptional skill of the spiritually-minded Baroque artist is particularly apparent in his depiction of saints (*The Ecstasy of St Bruno*, *The Vision of St Francis of Assisi*). *Tue 2.30pm–8pm, Wed–Sat 9am–8.30pm, Sun 9.30am–2.30pm | free admission for EU citizens | Plaza de Mina s/n*

ORATORIO DE LA SANTA CUEVA

A 17th-century house of prayer with a touchingly plain chapel to the Passion of Christ on the lower level and a monumental neo-Classical chapel on the first floor where three works by Goya are also to be found. *Tue–Sun 10am–1pm, Tue–Fri 4.30pm–7.30pm | admission 3 euros | C/ Rosario 10A*

ORATORIO DE SAN FELIPE NERI

One of the most beautiful Baroque churches in Andalucía with an elliptic floor plan. Shimmering natural light enters through windows in the cupola. It was here in 1811/12 that the *Cortes* (parliament) assembled to draw up Spain's first liberal constitution. A monument on the Plaza España is a reminder of the move towards democracy that was nipped in the bud. *Plaza San Felipe Neri*

TORRE TAVIRA 🌿

The lookout tower rises 45m (148ft) above the sea. A camera obscura projects moving pictures from the narrow streets below onto a screen. *Mid June–mid Sept daily 10am–8pm, otherwise 10am–6pm | admission 5 euros | C/Marqués del Real Tesoro 10 | www.torretavira.com*

FOOD & DRINK

FREIDURÍA LAS FLORES

A *freiduría* is a snack bar in the south of Andalucía. Instead of bangers and mash it sells fish and seafood. Tasty but fatty. *Plaza de las Flores | Budget*

INSIDER TIP LA GORDA TE DA DE COMER

This tapas restaurant with the unusual name 'The Fat Lady Serves your Food' is a popular and charming meeting place with reasonably-priced food in the Old Town. *Closed Sun | C/General Luque 1 (another branch is at C/Marqués de Valdeiñigo 4) tel. 9 56 28 94 93 | Budget–Moderate*

VENTORRILLO DEL CHATO

One of the best restaurants in the city. 2km (1¼mi) from the centre heading towards San Fernando. *Closed Sun | Vía Augusta Julia s/n | tel. 9 56 25 00 25 | Expensive*

MARCO POLO HIGHLIGHTS

⭐ **Cádiz**
The Old Town with its fine sandy beach → p. 76

⭐ **Sherry *bodegas***
The cathedrals of wine in Jerez de la Frontera → p. 84

⭐ **Museo Picasso Málaga**
Málaga's homage to its great son → p. 88

⭐ **Museo Carmen Thyssen**
Highlights of Spanish painting from the 19th and early 20th centuries in Málaga → p. 89

⭐ **Ronda**
A town that likes to keep its balance → p. 96

⭐ **Tarifa**
A surfers' paradise and Europe's southern-most town → p. 99

⭐ **The White Towns**
Gleaming pearls in the mighty mountains → p. 101

In the early evening on the sandy beach in Cádiz, the Playa de la Caleta

SHOPPING

Apart from the Plaza de las Flores with its flower market there is the neo-Classical market building, the *Mercado Central*, with a tempting range of culinary delicacies. The tuna caught on the Costa de la Luz is a speciality and is also available either deep-frozen or pickled at *Gadira, C/Plocia 8*.

BEACHES

The *Playa de la Caleta*, just 450m long, is to the west of the Old Town. The larger *Playa de la Victoria* (2.5km/1½mi) is on the south side of the strip of land connecting Cádiz with the rest of Andalucía.

SPORTS & ACTIVITIES

Ferries to *El Puerto de Santa María (duration 30 minutes, return ticket 4.55 euros | Avda. del Puerto | www.cmtbc.es)* depart from the harbour several times a day. The

● **INSIDER TIP** *Pepa Cádiz* also departs from here for tours around the Old Town and takes you to the sandy beach La Caleta *(1½ hrs., 12 euros | www.albarco. com)* at sunset.

WHERE TO STAY

INSIDER TIP ARGANTONIO
This charming little hotel in the Old Town quite rightly receives good reviews in Internet forums such as Tripadvisor. The rooms are a little small but tastefully and extremely cosily furnished. On top of this, it has a lovely situation and is good value for money. *15 rooms | C/Argantonio 3 | tel. 9 56 21 16 40 | www.hotelargantonio. com | Moderate*

PARADOR

Modern hotel between Castillo Santa Catalina and Parque Genovés. *149 rooms | Avda. Duque de Nájera 9 | tel. 9 56 22 69 05 | Expensive*

INFORMATION

OFICINA MUNICIPAL DE TURISMO
Paseo de Canalejas s/n | tel. 9 56 24 10 01 | www.cadizturismo.com, www.cadiz.es

CONIL DE LA FRONTERA

(142 B5) *(∅ D7)* **The traffic squeezes through Puerta de la Villa on the Plaza de España past guests sitting outside the cafés.**

Conil (pop. 22,000) on the Costa de la Luz, once the haunt of backpackers and language school students, has long since been discovered by tour operators and is slowly trying to become more up-market. The locals carry on their business as usual which adds to the attraction of the place. The best thing is the miles-long sandy beach more than 250m wide. To the far west are the *Calas del Cabo de Roche,* small sandy bays between tall cliffs.

FOOD & DRINK

FRANZISCO LA FONTANILLA
Beautifully situated, popular beach restaurant specialising in seafood. *Closed Wed except in July/Aug | Playa de la Fontanilla s/n | tel. 9 5 64 41 08 02 | Moderate*

SPORTS & ACTIVITIES

Rides of different lengths can be undertaken from the *Centro Hípico Pinares y Mar (Ctra. Fuente del Gallo-Cañada El Rosal | tel. 9 56 44 30 60 | mobile 6 49 98 62 75 | www.picaderopacheco.com).*
The long, sandy El Palmar beach, 2km (1¼mi) southeast of Conil, is popular among surfers.

WHERE TO STAY

FLAMENCO
Having been completely renovated recently this hotel is now more attractive then ever. Wonderful location slightly above Fuente del Gallo beach. *114 rooms | C/Sevilla 64–68 | tel. 9 56 44 07 11 | www.hipotels.com | Moderate–Expensive*

EL PÁJARO VERDE ☺
Simple but beautifully situated guesthouse right on the beach in El Palmar. Restaurant serving organic food. *8 rooms | El Palmar | tel. 9 56 23 21 18 | www.elpajaroverde.com | Budget*

INFORMATION

OFICINA DE TURISMO
C/Carretera 1 | tel. 9 56 44 05 01 | www.conildelafrontera.es

WHERE TO GO

MEDINA SIDONIA (142 C4) *(∅ D7)*
Whoever reaches the Plaza de la Iglesia Mayor high up above the town (pop.

LOW BUDGET

▶ When in Cádiz keep a lookout for a *freiduría* where fried fish to eat with your hands is sold at very reasonable prices.

▶ Visit *Cádiz Cathedral* for free from Tue–Fri 7pm–8pm, Sun 11.30am–1pm.

▶ ● Explore Málaga free of charge with a audio guide. MP3 players can also be rented at the tourist information centre on the Plaza de la Marina.

12,000, 37km/23mi northeast of Conil), having climbed the increasingly steep, narrow streets, is rewarded with a view over half the province of Cádiz. That just leaves the steps up the  tower of the *Iglesia de Santa María La Coronada (admission 2.50 euros)* from the 14th–17th centuries, from where you can enjoy a view stretching to the Atlantic and the Sierra de Grazalema, where the white villages gleam like snowy mountain peaks. A section of a Roman road has survived to this day. The Calzada Romana runs up to 4m (13ft) below the Calle Alamo and can now be seen along with the drainage system from Antiquity. *Conjunto Arqueológico Romano (Tue–Sun 10am–2pm, 4pm–6pm | admission 3.10 euros, combined ticket with the Iglesia de Santa María La Coronada 4 euros | C/Ortega).*

The tower at the Ermita de los Santos Mártires may possibly also be Roman.

What is probably Andalucía's oldest church, dating from the 7th century, can be found to the southwest of the town. The locals gather on the Plaza España in the *Restaurant Cádiz (Plaza España 13 | tel. 9 56 41 02 50 | Budget)*, for example, where you can eat outside. *Medina Sidonia (14 rooms | Plaza Llanete de Herederos 1 | tel. 9 56 41 23 17 | www.tugasa.com | Budget)* is a delightful hotel in the town. *Tourist information office: C/San Juan (near the Plaza de Abastos) | tel. 9 56 41 24 04 | medina sidonia.com.*

20km (12½mi) southeast, passing through green hilly country, is Benalup Casas Viejas. In 1933 anarchists instigated a revolution from here which they paid for with their lives.

The **INSIDER TIP** *Hotel Utopia (16 rooms | C/Dr. Rafael Bernal 32 | tel. 9 56 41 95 32 | www.hotelutopia.es | Expensive)* has been kept in the 1930s style and there is still

Water-spouting frogs on the Plaza España in Vejer de la Frontera

the feel of the bohemian Spanish liberals in the air in this unique hotel. Concerts and shows are regularly held in the restaurant *La Fonda*. The Nature Park *Alcornocales* with its lakes and cork oak forests is just a little further to the north. *Centro de Visitantes El Aljibe (A-2228)*.

INSIDER TIP NMAC ART PARK
(142 C5) (⌀ D8)

Sculptures by international artists such as Olafur Eliasson, Gregor Schneider and Sol Lewitt are on display in a grove of pine trees, cork oaks and olive trees. The NMAC Foundation Montenmedio Contemporary Art is an impressive museum combining art and nature *(Tue–Sun 10am–2pm, 5pm–8.30pm, in winter 10am–2.30pm, 4pm–6pm | on the N340, at km 42.5 between Tarifa and Vejer | admission 5 euros | www.fundacionnmac.org*

VEJER DE LA FRONTERA ●
(142 B5) (⌀ D7)

Vejer (pop. 13,000, 16km/10mi southeast of Conil) is Andalucía's 'white beauty', visible from a great distance on a 200m (656ft)-high hill. Courtyards full of flowerpots, *azulejos* and four water-spouting frogs in the shade of the palm trees on the Plaza de España. The *castillo* of Moorish origin is in the centre. A visit to the craft shop *Nuestra Artesanía* in the courtyard is well worthwhile.

Arabian-inspired dishes can be enjoyed on the shady terrace or in the romantic vaulted dining room at the restaurant *El Jardín del Califa (closed Sun afternoon in summer, Tue in winter | Plaza de España 12 | tel. 9 56 45 17 06 | Moderate)*. The adjoining hotel *Casa del Califa (26 rooms | tel. 9 56 44 77 30 | www.lacasa delcalifa.com | Budget–Moderate)* has lovely bright and atmospheric rooms. Juan Valdés' culinary and barbecuing skills are extremely popular among those

in the know. His open-air restaurant **INSIDER TIP** *La Castillería (daily, March–June only in the afternoon | tel. 9 56 45 14 97 | Moderate)* is a verdent oasis in the valley on the other side of the main road in the hamlet Santa Lucía.

The most recent hotel highlight, the elegant yet rustic *Hotel V (12 rooms | C/Rosario 11–13 | tel. 9 56 45 17 57 | www.hotelv-vejer. com | Expensive)*, shows how popular Vejer has now become. Guests in the twelve wonderful rooms are also treated to a waterfall.

Information: *Oficina Municipal de Turismo (Casa de la Cultura | C/Remedios 2 | tel. 9 56 45 17 36 | www.turismovejer.es)*. Vejer is just a few miles from the sea. To the southeast, through the Natural Park, is *Barbate* – a little town completely unaffected by tourism that is famous for its fleet of tuna fishing boats.

JEREZ DE LA FRONTERA

(142 B3) (⌀ D6) Jerez (pop. 210,000) shows what it has to the world on the

CITY WHERE TO START?
Signposts to the town centre (centro ciudad) are rare. And the places of interest in Jerez are rather scattered. Start at the **Alameda Cristina** where you can get a map of the town at the tourist information office. Drivers should head for the central underground car park Plaza El Arenal. You can also park on the Plaza Mamelón. The Santo Domingo stop next to the tourist information office is serviced by lines 2, 3, 4, 16 and 20.

Calle Larga (Long Street) – where people sit on ridiculously expensive terraces, a *fino* or a pint of beer in their hand, while others promenade up and down in their finery.

Jerez is famous for its fortified wine that foreigners call sherry – an anglicisation of the city's name – for its magnificent horses and for its flamenco tradition. But more than anything else Jerez is a surprise. It is a city full of sun-drenched elegance, full of hidden squares and monuments that have grown more beautiful with age. Jerez is however also a city with a high level of unemployment, day labourers and well-dressed gents. Jerez is Andalucía with both its good and bad sides.

SIGHTSEEING

ALCÁZAR

Enormous fortress with massive towers built during the Almohad dynasty (12th century). The interior includes Arabian baths, a small mosque and the Palacio de Villavicencio (18th century), that banned the Moorish flair to the far side of its walls. *Mon–Fri 9.30am–8pm (mid Sept–April 10am–6pm), Sat/Sun 9.30am–3pm | admission 5 euros, 7 euros incl. the camera obscura*

LA CARTUJA

The monastery, founded in 1476, lies beyond the city walls on the road to Algeciras. This marvel of ecclesiastic architecture was famous up until the 19th century for horse breeding. *Only open when services are held: Tue–Sat 7.30am Sun/Mon 5.30pm*. Craft shop selling items made in the monastery *Tue–Sat 11am–2pm*

CATEDRAL

Built in the 18th century this cathedral, with its imposing flights of steps, separate bell tower and mixture of styles with Gothic, Baroque and neo-Classical elements is unique. *Mon–Sat 10am–6.30pm | admission 5 euros*

CENTRO ANDALUZ DE FLAMENCO

The most important research centre into the art of the flamenco is housed in an 18th-century town palace. *Mon–Fri 9am–2pm | admission free | Plaza San Juan 1 | www.centroandaluzdeflamenco.es*

IGLESIA DE SAN DIONISIO

The church (15th century) in the local Mudéjar style is dedicated to the patron saint of the city *(admission only when services are held)*. It fronts the Plaza Asunción, one of the most beautiful squares in the city which is also flanked by the old town hall (*Cabildo Antiguo*, 16th century).

REAL ESCUELA ANDALUZA DE ARTE ECUESTRE

The Royal Andalusian School of Equestrian Art holds 18th-century style shows and horse fair galas that last just under two hours. *Visits during training sessions and to the Equestrian Arts and the Carriage Museums (visita temática) Mon, Tue (Jan, Feb) otherwise Wed, Fri 10am–2pm | admission 11 euros (concessions 6.50 euros) | without demonstrations (visita reducida) Tue, Thu 10am–2pm, in Aug also Fri | admission 6.50 euros (concessions 4.50 euros) | dressage show March–Dec Tue, Thu (Aug also Fri) 12 noon | admission 21–27 euros | Avda. Duque de Abrantes s/n | tel. 9 56 31 96 35 | www.realescuela.org*

SHERRY BODEGAS ★ ●

The famous *bodegas* (storage houses where sherry is aged and matured) run guided tours in English too. Advance booking by phone is more than advisable. *Domecq (Mon–Fri every hour, 10am–1pm, April–Sept also Sat 12 noon | admission*

8 euros | C/San Ildefonso 3 | tel. 9 56
15 15 00 | www.bodegasfundadorpedro
domecq.com).

González Byass (Tío Pepe | English tours
Mon–Sat 12 noon, 1pm, 2pm, 5.15pm
(Nov–May 5pm), Sun 12 noon, 1pm, 2pm |
admission from 12 euros | C/Manuel María
González 12 | tel. 9 56 35 70 00 | www.
bodegastiopepe.com).

Sandeman (English tours April–Oct Mon,
Wed, Fri 11.30am, 12.30pm, 1.30pm,
2.30pm, Tue, Thu 10.30am, 12 noon, 1pm,
2.15pm (Nov–March see website) | admis-
sion 7 euros | C/Pizarro 10 | tel. 9 56 31
29 95 | www.sandeman.com).

EL GALLO AZUL

Drink a glass of sherry, sample the tapas
and watch the comings and goings in
the pedestrian precinct. No visit to Jerez
is complete without a visit to 'The Blue
Cockerel'. The restaurant upstairs is more
expensive. *Closed Sun | C/Larga 2 | tel.
9 56 32 61 48 | Budget–Moderate*

INSIDERTIP▶ EL PATIO

There are several good restaurants in the
Calle San Francisco de Paula. El Patio is
cosy and friendly. Regional dishes. *Closed
Sun/Mon | C/San Francisco de Paula 7 |
tel. 9 56 34 07 36 | Moderate*

FOOD & DRINK

BAR JUANITO

The most famous tapas bar in Jerez is in
the city centre and is not cheap. *Closed
Sun evening | C/Pescadería Vieja 8/10 |
tel. 9 56 33 48 38 | Moderate*

SHOPPING

Sherry and hand-crafted items in the *Casa
del Jerez (C/Divina Pastora 1 | Local 3 | op-
posite the riding school)*. Excellent sherry
and brandy can be found in the Old Town
in the *bodega Rey Fernando de Castilla*

An interesting mixture of styles – the cathedral in Jerez de la Frontera

(Jardinillo 7–11 | www.fernadodecastilla. com). Items made of woven esparto grass are stocked in the *Casa del Mimbre (C/ Corredera 46).*

ENTERTAINMENT

Good places to start the evening are the bars on the Plaza Arenal and in the Calle Corredera.

TABLAO LAGÁ DE TÍO PARRILLA

One of the best flamenco stages in Andalucía. Performances Mon–Sat from 10.30pm, but you need to be there at least an hour in advance. Instead of an admission charge, the first drink costs a min. of 18 euros. *Plaza del Mercado s/n | tel. 9 56 33 83 34*

WHERE TO STAY

CHANCILLERÍA

Small, friendly and bright hotel in the Old Town. Nice roof terrace and an elegant restaurant, the *Sabores. 14 rooms | C/ Chancillería 21 | tel. 9 56 30 10 38 | www. hotelchancilleria.com | Moderate*

INSIDER TIP ▸ FÉNIX

In a quiet side street in the centre; clean, pretty, well furnished, low-priced rooms. What more could one want? *16 rooms | C/Cazón 7 | tel. 9 56 34 52 91 | www.hostal fenix.com | Budget*

HACIENDA SAN RAFAEL ☺

Fabulous *hacienda* approx. 40km (25mi) north of Jerez de la Frontera. The 200-year-old manor has large rooms, pools, a garden and a good restaurant. Breakfast is served in your room or on your own private terrace. Powered by solar energy. *Ctra. N-IV at km 594 | Las Cabezas de San Juan | tel. 9 54 22 71 16 | www.hacienda desanrafael.com | Expensive*

HOTEL PALACIO GARVEY

This contemporary, beautifully located hotel is housed in a 19th-century town palace. *16 rooms | Pl. Rafael Rivero 24 | tel. 9 56 32 67 00 | www.sferahoteles. com | Moderate–Expensive*

INFORMATION

OFICINA MUNICIPAL DE TURISMO
Plaza del arenal | tel. 9 56 33 88 74 | www. turismojerez.com

WHERE TO GO

EL PUERTO DE SANTA MARÍA
(142 B4) (*ᗰ D6*)

This town at the mouth of the Río Guadalete (pop. 89,000, 14km/8½mi southwest of Jerez) is a popular destination for Spaniards in the summer, attracted by the beaches and seafood – with one restaurants next to another vying for space around the Ribera del Marisco. The castle *San Marcos* (13th century) and the church *Iglesia Mayor Prioral* from the 15th and 17th centuries are in the Old Town.

Osborne, the *bodega* with the bull, is in the *Calle Moros 7 (guided tours regularly Mon–Fri (ring for times) | admission 8 euros | tel. 9 56 86 91 00).* The restaurant INSIDER TIP ▸ *Aponiente (closed Sun evening and Mon | Puerto Escondido 6 | tel. 9 56 85 18 70 | Moderate–Expensive)* is managed by the much-fêted chef Angel León and is certainly worth the detour. A delightful place to stay is the *Palacio San Bartolomé (11 rooms | C/San Bartolomé 21 | tel. 9 56 85 09 46 | www.palacio sanbartolome.com | Budget–Moderate).* This boutique hotel with a mini pool is in the centre of the Old Town.

Information: *Oficina de Turismo (Plaza del castillo | tel. 9 9 56 48 37 15 | www.turismo elpuerto.com)*

Nobody goes to bed early here – the Plaza del Cabildo in Sanlúcar de Barrameda

SANLÚCAR DE BARRAMEDA
(142 A3) (𝕄 C6)

Alfons Prince of Hohenlohe, whom the locals simply called 'Olé-Olé', had a luxury holiday complex built in Sanlúcar (pop. 67,000, 22km/14mi northwest of Jerez) at the mouth of the Guadalquivir, attracted by the wonderful position opposite the Doñana National Park. Information on the park is available at the *Centro de Visitantes Fábrica de Hielo (Bajo de Guía s/n | tel. 9 56 38 16 35)*. Tickets for boat trips to the *Doñana Natural Park (daily 10am, April/May, Oct also 4pm, June–Sept also 5pm | trip 17.25 euros | advanced booking recommended | tel. 9 56 36 38 13 | www.visitasdonana.com)* can be booked next door to the visitor centre. A number of rustic fish restaurants are located on the river where horseraces are held every year (mostly in Aug). An old-time favourite is the *Casa Balbino (Plaza del Cabildo 11 | tel. 9 56 36 05 13 | Budget–Moderate)* which serves more than 50 delicious types of tapas. A stroll through the Old

Town *(Barrio Alto)* will take you to the town hall in the neo-Mudéjar style from the 19th century, the church *Nuestra Señora de la O* (14th century) and the *Castillo de Santiago* (15th century). Try a *manzanilla* – the local sherry speciality – on the Plaza del Cabildo. *Posada de Palacio (34 rooms | C/Caballeros 11 | tel. 9 56 36 50 60 | www.posadadepalacio. com | Moderate–Expensive)* in the town centre is an Andalucían dream come true.

Information: *Oficina de Turismo (Calzada de la Duquesa Isabel | tel. 9 56 36 61 10 | www.sanlucardebarrameda.es)*

MÁLAGA

MAP INSIDE BACK COVER
(144 B–C5) (𝕄 H6) Fascinating museums, enchanting parks and a new harbour area – Málaga, Andalucía's second largest city (pop. 570,000), is becoming increasingly attractive.

The days when Málaga was virtually nothing more than a transfer point for holidaymakers on the Costa del Sol, are long gone. Since the long-awaited *Picasso Museum* opened its doors in 2003, old buildings in the historical centre have been renovated and more and more streets have gained a new lease of life and turned into pretty places for a stroll and to shop. Despite the continuing economic crisis things are happening here. New museums such as the *Museo Carmen Thyssen* and the *Museo Automovilístico* have been added to an already remarkable cultural landscape. When the remodelling of the *Museo de Málaga* in the Palacio de la Aduana has been completed, the Malagueños will have yet another reason to be proud of their city. But for the time being they can take pleasure in their recently revamped harbour area which, after Barcelona, is the most visited port of call on the Spanish mainland for cruise liners.

SIGHTSEEING

ALCAZABA

The Moorish fortification from the 11th century, the Alcazaba (from the Arabic *al-qasbah* meaning 'citadel'), was supposed to have been even more beautiful than the Alhambra in Granada. However, it is has now lost its former glory – what remains is merely a reminder of its original size. *Tue–Sun 8.30am–7pm, in summer 9.30am–8pm | admission 2.20 euros, Alcazaba and Gibralfaro 3.55 euros*

CASA NATAL PICASSO

A house on the Plaza de la Merced on the edge of the Old Town where Picasso is supposed to have lived as a young boy, was declared his birthplace. It now accommodates the Picasso Foundation and a small museum of exhibits focussing primarily on the artist's life as a youth. *Daily 9.30am–8pm, closed on public holidays | admission 2 euros | Plaza de la Merced 15 | www.fundacionpicasso.es*

CATEDRAL

La Manquita, 'the one-armed lady', is what the Malagueños call their cathedral. Its construction dragged on for more than 250 years (1528–1783) until the local residents said they had had enough of having to pay a special tax to finance all the pomp – and so it was completed without its second tower. Inside, the choir stalls, made by Pedro de Mena in the 17th century, and the organ with its 4000 pipes are noteworthy. *Mon–Fri 10am–6pm, Sat 10am–5pm | admission 5 euros*

GIBRALFARO ☼

Málaga's second Moorish fortress towers over the city from its hilltop site. It is linked to the Alcazaba by a walled-in path called the *Coracha*. A lovely footpath alongside the Coracha leads up onto the hill. A visit to the Gibralfaro (14th century) is worth it just for the view over the whole of Málaga and its harbour. *Daily 9am–8pm, in winter 6pm | admission 2.20, Gibralfaro and Alcazaba 3.55 euros, Sun free after 2pm*

MUSEO PICASSO MÁLAGA ★ ●

The Picasso Museum in Málaga is a must for all Picasso fans – and for those who

The Fundación Picasso is in the house where the artist was reputedly born

have not yet formed an opinion about the artist. Picasso's daughter-in-law and her son, Bernard, have given the museum more than 200 works – or lent them as permanent loans – covering all of the artist's creative periods. The collection is housed in the beautifully restored Palacio de Buenavista. *Tue–Thu, Sun 10am–8pm | Fri/Sat 10am–9pm | admission 9 euros | C/San Agustín 8 | www.museopicasso malaga.org*

MUSEO CARMEN THYSSEN ★

Work on the city's new cultural highlight, the Palacio Villalón in the Old Town of Málaga, lasted four years and swallowed 25 million euros. It is now home to 230 works of art from the collection of the Baroness Carmen Thyssen-Bornemisza, including 19th-century paintings and primarily Andalucían motifs by artists such as Joaquín Sorolla, Mariano Fortuny and Romero de Torres. *Tue–Sun 10am–8pm |*

admission 6 euros | C/Compañía 10 | www. carmenthyssenmalaga.org

FOOD & DRINK

ANTIGUA CASA DE GUARDIA

The most unspoilt *bodega* in Málaga has been in operation since 1840. Good wine and fresh seafood. *Daily | Alameda Principal 18 | Budget*

INSIDER TIP CITRÓN

Welcoming bar-restaurant with international dishes – a mixture of artists' café, restaurant and bar. Cheap menu of the day. *Daily | Plaza Merced 10 | tel. 9 52 22 63 99 | Budget–Moderate*

JOSÉ CARLOS GARCÍA ●

The star chef José Carlos García struck while the iron was hot and has now opened a super-deluxe restaurant in the new harbour area. His classic *Café de Paris* at *C/Vélez-*

Malaga 8 is still running too. Gourmet menus from 54 euros. *Tue–Sat evenings only, in winter also afternoons | Muelle 1 | tel. 9 52 00 35 88 | Expensive*

INSIDERTIP MANZANILLA

Dani García, one of Andalucía's best chefs, has opened an elegant bar in the Old Town. You can start off your evening sampling the delicious tapas while sipping a glass of *cava*. *Daily | C/Fresca 12 | tel. 9 52 22 68 51 | Moderate*

EL RESCOLDO

The *Calle de la Bolsa* is a good place to head for in the evening. *El Rescoldo* is well known for its delicious regional fare. Meat dishes such as *Secreto Ibérico,* a 'hidden' filet of Ibérico pork, can be especially recommended. *Daily | C/de la Bolsa 7 | tel. 9 52 22 69 19 | Moderate*

TABERNA EL PIMPI

Legendary tapas restaurant near the Picasso Museum. *Closed Mon afternoon | C/Granada 62 | tel. 9 52 22 89 90 | Moderate*

ENTERTAINMENT

Málaga's turbulent nightlife takes place around the *Plaza de la Merced*, in the *Calle Granada* and at the new harbour. In summer, also on the beaches and in the beach bars in the Pedregalejo district (*Chiringuito Miguelito*, for example, is very popular).

WHERE TO STAY

JUANITA

Small, well looked-after, quietly located hostel in the city centre. Many rooms have shared bathrooms. *14 rooms | C/Alarcón Luján 8 | tel. 9 52 21 35 86 | www.pension juanita.es | Budget*

INSIDERTIP ROOM MATE LOLA

The interior of this smaller Room-Mate designer hotel in Málaga looks like a combination of US design from the '50s and European Constructivism. The result is surprising and pretty cool. *50 rooms | C/Casas de Campos 17 | tel. 9 52 57 93 00 | www.room-matehotels.com | Moderate– Expensive*

POSADA DEL PATIO

Málaga's first and to date only 5-star hotel opened its glazed doors in 2010. Situated on the edge of the Old Town, it is in fact very central. The large rooms in a contemporary design harmonise well with the historical building. Small pool on the roof. *Pasillo Santa Isabel 7 | tel. 9 51 00 10 20 | www.vinccihoteles.com | Expensive*

INFORMATION

OFICINA MUNICIPAL DE TURISMO
Plaza de la Marina s/n (branches at Avda. Andalucia 1 and Plaza Merced 17) | tel. 9 52 92 60 20 | www.malagaturismo.com

OFICINA DE TURISMO DE LA JUNTA DE ANDALUCÍA
Pasaje de Chinitas 4 | tel. 9 51 30 89 11

WHERE TO GO

ANTEQUERA (144 B4) *(Ø H5)*

Slightly outside Antequera (pop. 45,000, 50km/31mi north of Málaga) are the *Dólmenes de Menga y Viera* (2500BC) and the *Dolmen del Romeral (Tue–Sat 9am–6pm, Sun 9.30am–2.30pm | admission free)* (1800BC). These megalithic burial chambers made of stones weighing several tonnes are exceptionally well preserved. To the south of the town is the fantastic karst landscape *Torcal de Antequera*. A 1-hour circular path (*Ruta*

Verde) takes you past the conical collection of rocks.

The Old Town of Antequera, with its wonderful Baroque churches, is also an inviting place for a stroll. From the Plaza San Sebastián walk up to the Plaza del Portichuelo and on to the ☆ *Castillo Árabe* and the *Real Colegiata de Santa María (Tue–Sat 10.30am–5.30pm, Sun 3pm)*. The *El Escribano (closed Sun evening and Mon | tel. 9 52 70 65 33 | Budget–Moderate)* with a sun terrace and regional specialities is on the Plaza de Santa María. Stay the night in the modern *Parador (60 rooms | Paseo García del Olmo | tel. 9 52 84 02 61 | www.parador.es | Moderate–Expensive)* that was revamped in 2008. Information: *Oficina Municipal de Turismo (Plaza de San Sebastián 7 | 9 52 70 25 05 | www.antequera.es)*

EL TORCAL (144 B5) *(ᗄ H6)*

Erosion and time have created a fantastic rocky landscape 15km (9½mi) south of Antequera. The karst formations in the *Paraje Natural El Torcal* are intriguing and can be explored by following one of the two hiking routes starting at the car park at the information centre. In good weather you can see as far as Africa from the ☆ *Mirador de las Ventillas*. The south side of the hill shelters a wolf sanctuary. *Lobo Park | daily 10am–6pm | admission 11 euros | Ctra. Antequera–Álora | A343 at km 16 | tel. 9 52 03 11 07 | www.lobopark.com*

GARGANTA DEL CHORRO (144 A4) *(ᗄ G6)*

58km (36mi) northwest of Málaga is the Garganta del Chorro or the Desfiladero de los Gaitanes, a spectacular gorge through which the Guadalhorce flows. Follow signs from Álora to El Chorro, then in the direction of Ardales. The footpath *Caminito del Rey* (the king's little path) through the gorge itself is closed due to its poor condition. Beyond El Chorro make a detour to the *ruins of Bobastro* with its 9th-century

The Dólmenes de Menga y Viera megalithic burial chambers in Antequera

chapel (when you seen the sign 'Iglesia Mozárabe 300m', stop, and continue from here on foot).

In Ardales there is a cave with rock drawings 24,000 years old *(www.cuevadeardales. com)*.

LAGUNA DE LA FUENTE DE PIEDRA
(144 A–B4) *(ⅅ G5)*

Thousands of brooding flamingos congregate from March to July on this shallow saltwater lake Fuente de Piedra, 69km (43mi) northwest of Málaga. The lagoon varies greatly in depth due to the natural flow of water.

TORREMOLINOS
(144 B6) *(ⅅ H6)*

It is difficult to imagine that this resort was a modest little village just half a century ago. Hotel complexes and apartment blocks as well as at least 300 bars, restaurants and discos are now densely packed in along the 7km (4½mi)-long beach. Whoever comes here on holiday does not want to visit any sites of interest – there aren't any here anyway – but is in search of the sun, a beach, fun and entertainment. Torremolinos (pop. 68,000 13km/8mi west of Málaga is a perfectly oiled package-holiday machine that accounts for one third of all the hotel accommodation on the Costa del Sol. Anyone overwhelmed by the enormous range of restaurants should first head towards *La Carihuela*. The popular *pescaítos fritos* – barbecued or fried fish – can be found in the old fishing district. A little off the beaten the track and 300m from La Carihuela beach is *La Luna Blanca (9 rooms | Pasaje Cerrillo 2 | tel. 9 52 05 37 11 | www.hotellalunablanca.com | Moderate– Expensive)* that can be highly recommended. Information: *Oficina de Turismo (Pl. Bals Infante 1 | and Pl. Independencia | tel. 9 52 37 95 11 | www.torremolinos.es)*

MARBELLA

(144 A6) *(ⅅ G7)* **It was not long ago that Marbella (pop. 139,000) was Spain's undisputed hotspot for the jet set – until Mallorca outstripped it.**

It still has a sophisticated atmosphere even if not everything is good taste. There is a lovely sandy beach in front of the battery of hotel and apartment blocks. Behind these is the old village with whitewashed houses and lots of flowers. At the centre is the Plaza de los Naranjos with its octagonal marble fountain and the 16th-century Town Hall. 6km (3¾mi) further west is *Puerto Banús* marina with its expensive restaurants, shops and discos.

FOOD & DRINK

INSIDER TIP ALTAMIRANO

It is loud, the television is blaring and the décor is nothing to write home about. But the guests are content which is hardly surprising judging by the tasty fish served here. *Closed Wed | Plaza Altamirano 4 | tel. 9 52 82 49 32 (no reservation possible) | Budget*

CALIMA

Andalucía's best restaurant. The head chef, Dani García, loves contrasts and has con-

---

CITY **WHERE TO START?**
The **Plaza de los Naranjos** in the Old Town and the area overlooking the sea are well worth seeing. The multi-storey car park next to the Park La Alameda lies right between the two. The bus lines 1, 2, 3, 6 and 7 go to the city centre. To reach the luxury marina Puerto Banús take a no. 1 bus from the Marbella Centro stop.

jured up three avant-garde and expensive menus. *Closed Sun/Mon | C/José Meliá | tel. 9 52 76 42 52 | www.restaurantecalima. com | Expensive*

INSIDER TIP EL GALLO

Even this still exists in Marbella – a restaurant serving plain, good Andalucían food at reasonable prices. Situated in the Old Town near the church Santo Cristo it belongs to the adjoining hotel that can also be recommended. *Closed Thu | C/Lobatas 46 | tel. 9 52 82 79 98 | Budget*

SANTIAGO

This classic restaurant on the sea promenade is still a good choice. The fresh seafood, fish and meat dishes are all excellent. *Daily | Paseo Marítimo 5 | tel. 9 52 82 45 03 | Expensive*

ENTERTAINMENT

There is an incredible number of bars, pubs and discos with a tendency more towards the sophisticated. The younger crowd meets up in the Old Town around Peral and Mesoncillo streets, on the Plaza de los Olivos or in the Calle Pantaleón. One of the most popular places in the Old Town is *Town House* in the Calle Álamo. Those who prefer things a little quieter should head for the bars in the Calle Camilo José Cela. The nightlife for the rich and beautiful takes place in Puerto Banús. Check things out in the *Guía Magazine Dia y Noche* (at the tourist information centre) or under *www.guiamarbella.com*

WHERE TO STAY

FUERTE MARBELLA | FUERTE MIRAMAR

There are two hotels, *Fuerte Marbella (263 rooms | Avda. El Fuerte s/n | tel. 9 52 86 15 00 | Expensive)* and *Fuerte Miramar (226 rooms | Plaza José Luque Manzano |*

Listening to music in the Old Town of Marbella

tel. 9 52 76 84 00 | Moderate–Expensive). Both are well located right on the beach and level with the Old Town. The rooms and facilities at both hotels are well maintained and comfortable. The older of the two, *Fuerte Marbella,* has the nicer garden and a little more character. *www.fuerte hoteles.com*

MARBELLA CLUB

The most famous hotel in town. The luxurious bungalow complex saw the beginning of the jet set era in Marbella in the 1960s. *121 rooms, 14 villas | Bulevar Príncipe von Hohenlohe | tel. 9 52 82 22 11 | www. marbellaclub.com | Expensive*

INSIDER TIP LA MORADA MÁS HERMOSA ☺

A tiny hotel with individually furnished rooms, some over two floors. Environmentally-friendly accessories and cotton

Fantastic formations – the Cueva de Nerja

Marbella), scattered like dice across the Sierra Bermeja, crowned by a Moorish ☆ *Castillo* (13th century) and with several restaurants on the Plaza España. The elegant golf hotel *Finca Cortesin (Ctra. Casares 2km/1¼mi | tel. 9 52 89 55 21 | www. fincacortesin.com | Expensive)* is one of Andalucía's top hotels. Very tastefully laid out with an exceptional restaurant and a variety of sporting possibilities. The rustic pub *Venta García (closed Mon | tel. 9 52 89 41 91 | Moderate)* serving crisp roast lamb is on the Ma 8300, 7km (4½mi) towards the coast. Information at the *Oficina de Turismo (C/Carrera 51 | tel. 9 52 89 55 21 | www.casares.es)*.

MIJAS (144 B6) (*ഗ G7*)

This beautiful town (pop. 80,000, 31km/ 19mi east of Marbella) attracts hordes of day-trippers. Stay a night at the *Hotel Mijas (204 rooms | C/Tamisa 2 | tel. 9 52 48 58 00 | www.trhhoteles.com | Moderate)* and climb up to the ☆ *Santuario de la Virgen de la Peña*, a 16th-century pilgrimage church, in the early morning. You can also treat your children to a trip on a donkey-drawn taxi *(leaving from the Plaza Virgen de la Peña | 10am–10pm, in winter 10am–6pm | from 10 euros)*. Information at the *Oficina de Turismo (Plaza Virgen de la Peña | tel. 9 52 58 90 34 | www.mijas.es)*.

bed linen underline the good-feel factor. The room in the tower and Room 2 with a roof terrace and lemon tree are particularly lovely. *6 rooms | C/Montenebros 16a | tel. 9 52 92 44 67 | www.lamoradamas hermosa.com | Budget–Moderate*

INFORMATION

OFICINA DE TURISMO
On the beach: *Glorieta de la Fontanilla s/n | tel. 9 52 77 14 42*. In the town hall: *Plaza de los Naranjos 1 | tel. 9 52 82 35 50 | www.marbella.es/turismo*

WHERE TO GO

CASARES (143 D–E4) (*ഗ F7*)

Picture-postcard village of whitewashed houses (pop. 5300, 56km/35mi west of

NERJA

(145 D5) (*ഗ J6*) A beautiful little town (pop. 22,000) on the eastern section of the Costa del Sol. But it is like sardines on the beach here in summer too.

The ☆ *Balcón de Europa* in the middle of *Nerja* is perched high above the sea on a rocky promontory and offers far-reaching views over the water from the wide viewing terrace. The little, romantic bays below are inviting and a reminder that Nerja was originally a fishing village before it became a tourist destination. Other beaches, some much wider, can be found both sides of the centre that, despite all the activity, has retained a pleasant village-like atmosphere.

SIGHTSEEING

CUEVA DE NERJA
Despite piped music and broad concrete paths it is still possible to marvel at the stalactites and stalagmites in this 4km (2½mi)-long cave. An impressive music festival is held here every year in July. *Daily 10am–2pm, 4pm–6.30pm, July/Aug without a break until 7.30pm | admission 8.50 euros | www.cuevadenerja.es*

FOOD & DRINK

INSIDER TIP LE RELAIS GOURMAND
Affordable French cuisine in Spain. This charming restaurant and its friendly owners has a strong fan community. *Daily | C/ Almirante 18 | tel. 9 52 52 23 22 | Moderate*

UDO HEIMER
This restaurant north of the centre is lovely and exclusive. The creations of the head chef Montserrat Mayor are a dream. *Closed Sun evening and Mon–Mi | C/ Andalucía 27 | tel. 9 52 52 00 32 | Expensive*

WHERE TO STAY

MAR AZUL
Cosy small hotel near the Playa de la Torrecilla. Most rooms have a view of the sea. *10 rooms | Avda. Mediterráneo 12 | tel. 9 52 52 41 91 | Budget–Moderate*

PARADOR
Rooms with balconies overlooking the sea. Lift to the beach. *73 rooms | C/ Almuñécar 8 | tel. 9 52 52 00 50 | Expensive*

INSIDER TIP PARAÍSO DEL MAR
Lovingly and luxuriously furnished with a sea view. *18 rooms | Prolongación de Carabeo 22 | tel. 9 52 52 16 21 | www.hotel paraisodelmar.es | Moderate–Expensive*

INFORMATION

OFICINA DE TURISMO
C/Carmen 1 | tel. 9 52 52 15 31 | www.nerja. org

WHERE TO GO

FRIGILIANA (145 D5) (*Ø J6*)
Only 6km (3¾mi) north of Nerja you can leave the Costa del Sol behind you just for a day. The higher you climb through the narrow streets of this completely white-washed village (pop. 3300) the more you will feel transported back to the days of the Moors.

El Ingenio, the largest building at the foot of the Barrio Mudéjar, the prettiest part of the village, was the seat of the country gentleman Manrique de Lara from 1508 onwards. Apart from lots of ceramic items, you can buy sugar cane honey here.

The *Fábrica de Miel de Caña* is unique in Europe. A place to eat with a view is the *El Mirador (closed Tue, June–Aug evenings only | C/Santo Cristo 29 | tel. 9 52 53 32 91 | Moderate)*. *Las Chinas (7 rooms | Plaza Capitán Cortés 14 | tel. 9 52 53 30 73 | Budget)* is a simple but well-run guest-house with a good restaurant. Frigiliana is also a good base for a visit to the Natural Park *Tejadas y Almijara*. 154mi² of this mountainous area are protected. Information available at the *Oficina de Turismo (Cuesta del Apero | tel. 9 52 53 42 61 | www.frigiliana.es)*

INSIDER TIP MARO (145 D5) (*Ø J6*)
This whitewashed village (pop. 800; 4km/ 2½mi east) is still very much an insider

tip. That may be because you have to walk a bit to the local beach. Village life is peaceful and has remained unchanged. There is very little tourism here that could have a negative effect. The centre is the ☀ terrace next to the church *Virgen de las Maravillas* from where there are lovely views. ☺ *Casa Maro (9 rooms | C/ Maravillas | tel. 6 27 95 84 56 | www.hotel-casa-maro.com | Budget–Moderate)* has Mediterranean-style apartments with sea views and an organically maintained swimming pool.

RONDA

(143 E3) *(Ш F6)* Romantic ⭐ Ronda (pop. 37,000) is perched on a rocky plateau with a vertical drop of 165m (541ft). The town is divided by a deep ravine (Spanish: *tajo*).

The ☀ *Puente Nuevo*, a spectacular masterpiece of 18th-century engineering, links the old part of Ronda (called *La Ciudad*, 'the town') and the now not-so-new part *(El Mercadillo,* 'the little market') north of the *tajo* that has evolved since the 16th century. The Romans and the Moors in particular, who remained unconquered until 1485 when defeated by the Catholic monarchy, left their mark. Present-day 'romantic' Ronda, is a town of the 18th century however, praised by poets and writers, including Ernest Hemmingway who used the town as a setting for this novel *For Whom the Bell Tolls.*

SIGHTSEEING

BAÑOS ÁRABES

The largest Arabian bath complex and the best preserved in Spain, dating from the 13th/14th centuries, lies at the bottom of

The Puente Nuevo, the 'New Bridge' links the two parts of Ronda

the ravine near the Puente San Miguel. *Mon–Fri 10am–7pm, in winter 6pm, Sat/Sun 10am–3pm | admission 3 euros*

IGLESIA SANTA MARÍA LA MAYOR

Ronda's main church is on the most beautiful square in the town, the *Plaza Duquesa de Parcent*, planted with palms and bay trees that provide shade. Inside the entrance a richly decorated prayer niche that once formed part of the mosque that stood on this site, leads off to one side. In the church, built after the Christian conquest of Ronda, Gothic and Renaissance elements clash unforgivingly with one another. *June–Sept daily 10am–8pm, Oct–May daily 10am–6pm | admission 4 euros*

LA MINA

The 18th-century town palace *Casa del Rey Moro (April–Oct daily 10am–8pm,*

otherwise 6.30pm | admission 4 euros)* on the edge of the *tajo* is rather run-down but is intriguing. A Mooorish king had a complicated arrangement of steps hewn inside the rock in the 14th century which lead 60m (197ft) down into the depths below. The *Mina de Agua* (lit: 'water mine') served as both a fountain and a defence system.

PALACIO DE MONDRAGÓN

One of Ronda's beautiful town palaces with inner courtyards in the Mudéjar style. It is now the *Museo Municipal (Mon–Fri 10am–7pm, in winter 6pm, Sat/Sun 10am–3pm | admission 3 euros)* with replicas of Stone Age burial chambers and caves.

PLAZA DE TOROS

The bullring (1785) is the oldest in Spain and the only one where the two-tiered rows of seats, surrounding an unusually large arena, are completely roofed over. The adjoining *Museo Taurino (April–Sept daily 10am–8pm, Oct–March daily 10am–6pm | admission 6.50 euros | www.rmcr.org)* provides a good introduction to the history of bullfighting.

PUERTA DE ALMOCÁBAR

The gate with pointed horseshoe arches (13th century) at the southern end of La Ciudad is a remnant of the Moorish fortifications. The Catholic monarchs Ferdinand and Isabella built the church Espíritu Santo (1505), the simplicity of which makes it particularly beautiful, right next to it on the foundations of a Moorish castle. *Mon–Sat 10am–2pm | admission 1 euro*

FOOD & DRINK

INSIDER TIP **FAUSTINO**
Appealing tapas bar with plain but good food in the restaurant area for just 6 euros. Very popular and always full. *Closed Mon |*

C/Santa Cecilia 4 | tel. 9 52 19 03 07 | *Budget*

PEDRO ROMERO
This typically rustic restaurant has been something of an institution for years. Specialities include oxtail soup – a real must. *Daily | Virgen de la Paz 18 | tel. 9 52 87 11 10 | Moderate–Expensive*

TRAGABUCHES
Exceptional creations of modern Spanish cuisine can be enjoyed in minimalistic surroundings. Benito Gómez is also in charge of the food served in the tapas restaurant *Tragatapas (Calle Nueva). Closed Sun evenings and Mon | C/José Aparicio 1 | tel. 9 52 19 02 91 | Expensive*

WHERE TO STAY

ALAVERA DE LOS BAÑOS
Below the Old Town near the Arabian baths, this tastefully decorated hotel is an ideal place to relax thanks to its peaceful location, its garden, pool and library. Tasty breakfast. *9 rooms | C/San Miguel | tel. 9 52 87 91 43 | www.alaveradelosbanos.com | Moderate*

REINA VICTORIA
From outside, this venerable old hotel from 1906 is as it has always been, with lovely views and a wonderful garden. Inside, it has been completely revamped and turned into a modern boutique hotel with a spa. The one negative point – the old museum room dedicated to the Bohemian-Austrian poet Rainer Maria Rilke has disappeared. *95 rooms | C/Jerez 25 | tel. 9 52 87 12 40 | www.hoteles-catalonia.com | Moderate–Expensive*

INSIDER TIP RONDA
This tiny family-run hotel is slightly above the *Casa del Rey Moro*. Breakfast is served

in the tastefully modern rooms. *5 rooms | Rueda Doña Elvira 12 | tel. 9 52 87 22 32 | www.hotelronda.net | Budget–Moderate*

VIRGEN DEL ROCÍO
Pleasant, well furnished, cheap guesthouse in the Old Town. *15 rooms | C/Nueva 18 | tel. 9 52 87 74 25 | www.hostalvirgendelrocio.com | Budget*

INFORMATION

OFICINA DE TURISMO
Paseo de Blas Infante s/n | tel. 9 52 18 71 19 | www.turismoderonda.es

WHERE TO GO

CUEVA DE LA PILETA
(143 E3) (*ꭲ F6*)
The prehistoric caves, 27km (17mi) southwest of Ronda, boast rock drawings 27,000 years old. *1-hour guided tours daily 10am–1pm, 4pm, 5pm | admission 8 euros*

GAUCÍN (143 D4) (*ꭲ F7*)
This pretty village of whitewashed houses (pop. 2000) in the Serranía de Ronda is firmly in British hands. Lots of artists live here and their works are on show in the many galleries and studios. This is a lovely place to spend a few days; e.g. at the hotel INSIDER TIP *Casablanca (7 rooms | C/Teodoro de Molina 12 | tel. 9 52 15 10 19 | www.casablanca-gaucin.com | Expensive). La Fructuosa (Fri/Sat evening | C/Convento 67 | tel. 9 52 15 10 72 | www.lafructuosa.com | Moderate)* is a stylish restaurant in an old wine cellar that also has five hotel rooms *(Moderate)* with lovely views. This is also true of the ⚓ Castillo de Águila *(daily 10am–1.30pm, 4pm–7.30pm)* that was built in the late 9th century. Information: *Oficina del Turismo (Paseo Ana Toval | tel. 9 52 15 10 00 | www.gaucin.es)*

TARIFA

(143 D6) (⚏ E8) ★ Tarifa (pop. 18,000) was named after the Berber general Tariq ibn Ziyad, who crossed the Strait of Gibraltar in 710AD and paved the way for the Conquest of Hispania.

The atmosphere here is a bit like Goa or Australia, with a big dollop of Moorish history thrown in for good measure. Here, at the southern-most tip of Spain, the wind blows through the straits and can make bathing pretty unpleasant. But surfers think its great – Tarifa is a 'high wind area'.

SIGHTSEEING

CASTILLO DE GUZMÁN EL BUENO

Well-preserved Moorish fortress from the 10th century. Christians conquered the town in 1292 but the Arabs were not beaten easily. During a siege they took the son of the governor, Alfonso Pérez de Guzmán, captive. But instead of leaving Tarifa to the Moors in return for his son, Guzmán threw his sword from the tower for them to kill his son. That resulted in him being called *El Bueno*, 'the Good'. *Tue–Sat 11am–2pm, 5pm–7pm, Sun 11am–2pm | admission 2 euros*

PLAZUELA DEL VIENTO ☄

From the 'little windy square' – that certainly lives up to its name – you have a lovely view across to Africa, 20km (12½mi) away.

FOOD & DRINK

MISIANA BAR

Good breakfasts, nice café, cool lounge in the evening. *Daily | C/Sancho IV El Bravo 16 | tel. 9 56 62 74 14*

MORILLA

This bar restaurant on the *Plaza Oviedo* is the town's front room and is always

Tarifa, the most southerly point of Spain, is a hotspot for surfers

packed. Simple and traditional cooking. *Daily | C/Sancho IV El Bravo 2 | tel. 9 56 68 17 57 | Budget*

SPORTS & ACTIVITIES

Wind and kite surfing, stand-up paddling, (wave) surfing, riding, mountain biking, climbing, paragliding – everything is possible here. Details from the tourist information centre. 1 or 2-day trips to neighbouring Tangier in Morocco are available at the harbour *(FRS operates crossings several times a day | tel. 9 56 68 18 30 | day-trip 59 euros | www.frs.es)*. Boat trips with whalewatching: *Whale Watch Tarifa (bookings tel. 9 56 62 70 13 | www.whale watchtarifa.net)* and *firmm (tel. 9 56 62 70 08 | www.firmm.org | 30 euros)*.

WHERE TO STAY

ALAMEDA
Simple hotel near the *castillo*. *27 rooms | Paseo Alameda 4 | tel. 9 56 68 11 81 | www.hostalalameda.com | Budget– Moderate*

DOS MARES
The nicest hotel on the *Los Lances* surfing beach, in the Andalucían style, with first-class restaurant. *48 rooms | Ctra. N340, at km 79.5 | tel. 9 56 68 40 35 | www.dos mareshotel.com | Moderate–Expensive*

POSADA LA SACRISTÍA
Rooms in small, boutique-style hotels are much in demand in Tarifa. *La Sacristía* is certainly one of the nicest such hotels with individually designed rooms with a special flair of their own, a small sun terrace, a lounge restaurant and relaxing massages to make you feel completely spoilt. *10 rooms | C/San Donato 8 | tel. 9 56 68 17 59 | www.lasacristia.net | Expensive*

INFORMATION

OFICINA DE TURISMO
Paseo de la Alameda s/n | tel. 9 56 68 09 93 | www.aytotarifa.com/Turismo/ingles. htm, www.aytotarifa.com/turismo

WHERE TO GO

INSIDER TIP ► BOLONIA ●
(142 C6) (*Ø E8*)
A sweeping bay with a fine sandy beach (the most beautiful far and wide), a few *hostales* and *chiringuitos,* 23km (14mi) northwest of Tarifa. *Los Jerezanos (25 rooms | Lentiscal 5 | tel. 9 56 68 85 92 | Moderate)* is a family-run hotel and restaurant right on the beach. Next to it are the ruins of the small Roman settlement Baelo Claudia with a circular route for visitors *(June–Sept Tue–Sat 10am–8pm, Oct–May Tue–Sat 10am–7pm, Sun 10am– 2pm | free admission for EU citizens)*; flyers available at the entrance.

INSIDER TIP ► CASTELLAR DE LA FRONTERA (143 D5) (*Ø E7*)
Magical. 70 houses jostle for space within the walls of this Moorish fortress (13th/ 14th centuries), built on the top of a hill. Cars have to be left outside the castle gate (on the A405 follow the signs for Castillo de Castellar, 49km/30mi northeast of Tarifa). You only need a few minutes to explore the few cobbled lanes full of climbing plants and to take in the view from the ✲ *mirador* of the reservoir below. In 1971 the former residents of the *castillo* moved out and built a new village down on the plain. Escapists then moved into the empty houses. A cosy restaurant and your own little cottage can now be found in *Castillo de Castellar (9 houses sleeping 2–6 | restaurant daily | C/Rosario 3 | tel. 9 56 69 31 50 | www. tugasa.com | Moderate–Expensive)*.

GIBRALTAR (143 D5–6) (*∅ F8*)

Crossing the border from Andalucía you enter another world. Befittingly you must have your passport with you. Be prepared for extensive and meticulous searches. Gibraltar (41km/25½mi northeast of Tarifa, pop. 29,000) is very British – the Rock being a British Overseas Territory since 1713. Some 7 million visitors come here every year to explore the massive Rock that is home to the famous apes and Main Street with its duty-free shopping. It is well worth visiting the ☀ *Upper Rock Nature Reserve* and *St Michael's Cave* (with stalactites and stalagmites), the *Great Siega Tunnels* (defence system from the end of the 18th century), the *Apes' Den* (where the famous Barbary macaques leap around) and to take in the view. The reserve is best reached by cable car *(Mon–Sat 9.30am–5.15pm | return adult fare 14.70 euros; incl. Nature Reserve 28.70 euros)*. The currency in Gibraltar is Pounds Sterling, but many prices are given in euros. *Dolphin watching (approx. 35 euros/person)* is also very popular. There are several companies operating mostly out of Marina Bay. It you don't fancy fish 'n chips, try elegant *Nuno's (Catalan Bay | tel. +3 50 20 07 65 01 | Expensive)*, in what is probably the best hotel in the Territory – *The Caleta Hotel*. Or spend a night in Gibraltar in style at the *Bristol Hotel (60 rooms | Cathedral Square 8/10 | tel. +3 50 20 07 68 00 | www. bristolhotel.gi | Moderate)*, a historical, colonial-style building in a central location. If you intend staying until the evening, drive to Gibraltar by car. The wait at customs on the way back is not usually very long. Or else park just before the border on the Spanish side in *La Línea*. From there Main Street is a 15 min. walk or hop in a taxi after crossing the border. Customs regulations are those of a non-EU country – goods to the value of 300 euros

Gibraltar's Barbary apes

(430 euros for those arriving by air or sea), 200 cigarettes and 1 litre of spirits are duty free.

Information: *Gibraltar Tourist Board (Cathedral Sq. | tel. +3 50 4 50 00 | www. gibraltar.gov.uk/holiday.php)*

THE WHITE TOWNS

★ *Los pueblos blancos* **– surreal, gleaming blobs of white dotted all over the green, brown or grey Andalucían countryside.**

The more or less perfectly whitewashed houses reflect the midday sun and prevent the rooms inside from turning into ovens. Thanks to an especially clever idea to promote tourism, the white villages and little towns between Ronda and Arcos de la Frontera have virtually become a brand name.

THE WHITE TOWNS

ARCOS DE LA FRONTERA
(142 C3) (*ⴑ E6*)

The first time you reach the Plaza del Cabildo in the heart of the town (pop. 32,000) you will probably want to go up to the ☀ *Mirador de la Peña Nueva*. The view over the edge is simply breathtaking. Arcos is like a white slab on an ochre-coloured rocky cliff that, to the southwest, drops vertically 160m (525ft) to the *Río Guadalete* below. Opposite the *mirador* on the other side of the square is the basilica *Santa María* (15th century) with its huge ☀ bell tower. The *town hall* lines the left-hand side of the square (with a beautiful *artesonado* ceiling), with the more than 1000-year-old Moorish castle behind. *Oficina Municipal de Turismo (tel. 9 56 70 22 64 | www.turismoarcos.es)*. On the right-hand side is the *Parador (24 rooms | tel. 9 56 70 05 00 | Moderate–Expensive)*. The balconies look straight down to the bottom of the cliff.

The *Calle de los Escribanos* with its stone arches leads down the side of the Parador to the labyrinthine streets of the Old Town. After a short distance you will reach the *Convento de Mercedarias Descalzas (1642, Baroque retable, daily 8.30am–2.30pm, 5pm–7pm | Plazuela de Botica 2)*. INSIDER TIP The nuns sells little home-made cakes through a hatch. Accommodation is available at the *Casa Grande (7 rooms | Maldonado 10 | tel. 9 56 70 39 30 | www.lacasagrande.net | Budget–Moderate)*. This town house full of character is right on the cliff edge. The *patio* and the beautifully furnished library are a delight. The most unusual restaurant in town is the ☺ INSIDER TIP *Taberna de Boabdil (daily | Paseo de Boliches 35 | tel. 9 56 70 51 91 | Budget)*. It is in a cave and the owner claims it was used as a synagogue after the Reconquista. The chef calls his creations 'a fusion of cultures that live in Arco' and some of his ingredients come from his own organic garden. Those who prefer things a little more stylish will find what they are looking for in the Parador restaurant *El Corregidor (daily | Plaza del Cabildo | tel. 9 56 70 05 00 | Expensive)*.

INSIDER TIP BENADALID
(143 E4) (*ⴑ F7*)

The Moorish fortress still dominates the area up above the valley, but its walls now enclose a cemetery of white sepulchral niches. Benadalid (pop. 270) is an enchanting spot on the Serranía de Ronda. On the main road there is the only place in the area to stay – simple but well maintained – *Aguayar (5 rooms | Ctra. A369, at km 25 | tel. 9 52 15 27 68 | Budget)*

GRAZALEMA
(143 D3) (*ⴑ F6*)

The little white town (pop. 2200) lies at the foot of the spiky Peñón Grande (Large Rock). Geographically and touristically it is the centre of the Natural Park *Sierra de Grazalema*. Everything a tourist could wish for can be found on the *Plaza de España* – shops (beautiful hand-woven lambswool cloth), bars and restaurants. Located in the middle of hot Andalucía, this is the spot that actually has the most rainfall in all of Spain, much to the good of the many Spanish firs that look like perfect Christmas trees. *Fuerte Grazalema (77 rooms | Baldío de los Alamillos | A372, km 53 | tel. 9 56 13 30 00 | www.fuerte. com | Moderate)* is a 4-star hotel which is excellent value for money. It lies outside the village and has a pool with a fantastic view of the mountains. A lovely, less expensive hotel is *Casa de las Piedras (30 rooms | C/Las Piedras 32 | tel. 9 56 13 20 14 | www.casadelaspiedras.org | Budget)*. Information: www.grazalema.es

SETENIL DE LAS BODEGAS
(143 E3) (*ω F6*)

This spectacular little town (pop. 3000) is squeezed into the narrow gorge of the Río Guadalporcún. Only the façade of many houses is actually visible, the rest being dug into the rock behind. The ☀ tower of the Moorish fort, located at the highest point in the town, dominates the surrounding area and, when not locked, provides a view that extends as far as Olvera. Setenil credits itself with having invented tapas and even has a *Ruta del Tapeo*. INSIDERTIP ▶ *La Tasca (closed Mon and evenings, except Sat | C/Cuevas del Sol 71 | Budget)* and the *Restaurante El Mirador (closed Mon | tel. 6 59 54 66 26 | Budget)* can be recommended. The hotel *El Almendral (28 rooms | Ctra. Setenil–Puerto del Monte s/n | tel. 9 56 13 40 29 | www.tugasa.com | Budget)* has a pretty location on the edge of the town (on the Ronda road). It is good value and has a pool.
Information: *Oficina de Turismo (C/Villa 2 | tel. 9 56 13 42 61, 6 59 54 66 26 | www.setenil.com)*

ZAHARA DE LA SIERRA
(143 D3) (*ω F6*)

Zahara (pop. 1600) is basically one steep road, built up the side of a rocky outcrop with the Moorish ☀ *Torre de Homenaje* (13th century) at the top. The restaurant and tapas bar *Los Naranjos (daily | tel. 9 56 12 33 14 | Budget)* is located in the village centre. Part of the hotel *Arco de la Villa (17 rooms | Camino Nazarí s/n | tel. 9 56 12 32 30 | www.tugasa.com | Budget)* is in the old fortress. Information, also on hiking routes, rides, canoe trips: *Oficina de Información del Parque Natural (Plaza del Rey 3 | tel. 9 56 12 31 14). www.zaharadelasierra.es, www.zaharacatur.com*

Yes, it's true – Grazalema really is the rainiest spot in Spain

TRIPS & TOURS

The tours are marked in green in the road atlas, the pull-out map and on the back cover

1 GREEN ANDALUCÍA

A round trip from Sevilla to the Doñana National Park and the Sierra de Aracena, with visits to sites associated with Columbus. For this 400km (250mi)-long stretch, plan two overnight stops.

Leave Sevilla on the A49 to Huelva. Turn off this road at km 48 and follow signs to P. N. Doñana. The dead straight road crosses the flat alluvial plain on the west-hand side of the Guadalquivir. Observe the speed limit as speed cameras are often set up here. The first stop is in El Rocío

→ p. 47. Sandy trails lead through the village that is visited by up to a million people at Whitsun. The church of the 'Virgin of the Dew' however attracts pilgrims all year round. The Doñana National Park → p. 45 starts beyond El Rocío. Just before reaching Matalascañas turn off onto a narrow road to El Acebuche → p. 46 visitor centre. From here you can follow a nature trail through the area near the park boundary or book a tour to the heart of the national park. The green 4 × 4 buses depart in the summer Mon–Sat at 8.30am and 5pm; in winter Tue–Sun at 8.30am and 3pm. This is the only way to access the protected area in the middle of the park

Photo: Guadix Cathedral and the surrounding area

Our suggested tours by car, by bike or on foot take you from village to village through varied scenery

and to see its wildlife. Carry on along the A494 towards Mazagón – if you fancy a dip in the sea stop at the **Cuesta Maneli** → p. 47 car park and walk across the dunes to the beach. The **Parador** → p. 47 in Mazagón can be recommended for the first night's stop. On leaving Mazagón turn off to **Palos de la Frontera** and **La Rábida** → p. 45 where you can clamber around replicas of Columbus' ships. In *La*

Rábida monastery imagine Columbus trying to win over the padres for his idea and find a way to gain an audience with Queen Isabela. Via Moquer and Niebla, which both warrant a short stop, carry on along the by-road HV5111 to Valverde del Camino, passing through gentle hilly country.

The route now becomes hillier and twistier. 55km (34mi) beyond Valverde take the turning signposted to Aracena → p. 32. Keep an eye out for somewhere to stay the night and then sample the local, world-famous speciality, Ibérico ham. The ultimate is jamón Ibérico de bellota from the dark-coloured breed of pig. In the last few months of their short lives in the *dehesas* (oak forests used for grazing) between Andalucía and the Extremadura, they feed solely on acorns. When in the forested Sierra de Aracena, a hike is a must. A short walk of around 6km (3¾mi) will take you from Almonaster la Real to Cerro San Cristóbal. Almonaster la Real → p. 35 is one of the prettiest villages in the area. Fuenteheridos and Alájar → p. 35 should not be missed either. Castaño del Robledo is famous for its chestnut forests. Just before reaching Alájar you pass the Ermita Reina de los Ángeles (follow signs to Pena de Arias Montano), a popular destination with a restaurant, small pottery shop and a view of Alájar. On the way back to Sevilla, a detour to the little village of Zufre → p. 36 is well worthwhile. Here, not far from the regional capital, you can marvel at the ruins of Itálica → p. 57. A stroll through the site will show you how comfortably the Romans lived and how cultivated they were even in such a far-flung province as Hispania.

2 THE ANDALUCÍAN DESERT

 Large expanses of east Andalucía are nothing but stones and sun. Plan two days for the 250km (155mi) from Mojácar to Cazorla and one more day for the 100km (62mi) from Cazorla to Jaén.

From San José in the Cabo de Gata Natural Park → p. 62, where you might want to have a quick swim on the Playa del Mónsul in the morning, you travel through barren volcanic scenery, past the old gold mine in Rodalquilar and, beyond the park boundary, you will see huge greenhouses where vegetables for the supermarkets in central and northern Europe are grown. The narrow, twisty mountain road AL3107 takes you via the pleasant little town of Níjar to Europe's only desert – El Desierto de Tabernas. Just before reaching the A92 to Granada you pass the 'Western towns' → p. 63, where several film classics were made. Following the A92 to Guadix you have a wonderful view of the Sierra de los Filabres and the Sierra Nevada. Near Calahorra, the Renaissance castle of the same name is on the left, set off against the frequently snow-covered eastern foothills of the Sierra Nevada. The vast plains are being increasingly covered in solar collectors which belong to what is at present the largest solar power station in Europe. Film buffs should not miss visiting the little station in La Calahorra where

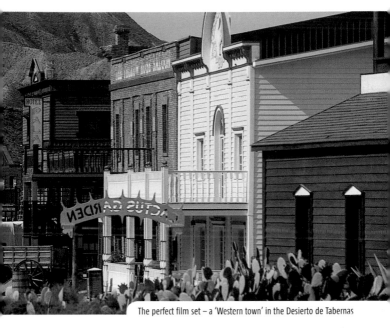

The perfect film set – a 'Western town' in the Desierto de Tabernas

the opening scene in Once Upon a Time in the West was filmed.

Guadix → p. 72 is not only interesting because of its cave dwellings but also for its centre with its massive cathedral and the lovely Plaza de la Constitución. The romantic hotel **Abentofail** (C/Abentofail | tel.9 58 66 92 81 | www.hotelabentofail. com | Budget–Moderate), which also has a good restaurant, is just a short walk from here in the Old Town. From Guadix, take the A92N and, after 25km (16mi) near Baúl, turn off to Bácor-Olivar (junction 321). This is where the most adventurous part of the route begins, cutting right across the INSIDER TIP Altiplano de Granada at an altitude of 1000m (3280ft) through a remote steppe region. All of a sudden a reservoir, the **Embalse del Negratín,** appears out of nowhere. The road crosses the dam with the restaurant **El Pantano del Negratín** (closed Mon |

tel. 9 58 34 22 65 | Budget) beyond, overlooking the shimmering turquoise water – a perfect place for a break. The scenery changes abruptly on crossing the border into Jaén province, with nothing but olive trees to the left and right. On the long stretch between Pozo Alcón and Quesada take a by-road that winds its way up through pine forests to Puerto de Tiscar – the southern tip of the Sierra de Cazorla. The view from the pass over the olive groves is absolutely breathtaking. Head downhill passing through Quesada and then turn right up a side road to **Cazorla** → p. 63. After such a fill of dramatically beautiful scenery your eyes will need a rest and your stomach may be calling for attention. How about a night in the secluded Parador in Cazorla? Here you will find both a menu with local specialities and total peace and quiet. The following day is reserved for a bit of culture. Leaving

Capileira, one of the famous *pueblos blancos* in the Sierra Nevada

Cazorla through the sheer endless rows of olive trees you will arrive at the Renaissance towns of **Baeza and Úbeda** → p. 74. And if that's not enough culture for you, take a look at **Jaén Cathedral** → p. 74 too to finish, as well as the sea of olive trees from the castillo.

3 HIKE FROM VILLAGE TO VILLAGE

This medium-to-difficult hike leads through the beautiful Valle de Poqueira to the Alpujarras. Difference in altitude: about 800m (2625ft); hiking time only: 5 hours. The 12km (7½mi) route links the picturesque villages of Bubión, Pampaneira and Capileira.

Villages cling to the slopes of a deep gorge in what is arguably the most beautiful valley in the western Alpujarras, the **Valle de Poqueira** → p. 72. The snow on the peaks of the Sierra Nevada remains until the early summer. **Capileira** → p. 72 is

the highest village in the valley and the starting point of this hike. The more sporty may want to climb **Mulhacén** → p. 73 from here, which can be well recommended providing the weather is both good and stable and you have the appropriate equipment. Our more gentle tour however takes you through the valley with a modest difference in altitude of 800m (2625ft). In Capileira take the Calle del Castillo in the upper part of the village to the former settlement of **La Cebadilla**. The path follows the Río Poqueira and crosses it, after about 1 hour, beyond La Cebadilla. On the west side of the valley, the path then returns in the opposite direction. There is a short uphill stretch to start with, before arriving at the wider path through the valley. After about 45 mins. you will re-cross the Río Poqueira via the Puente Buchite and then back again over the Puente de Chiscar, leaving Capileira on the far side of the valley. The path, that is not always clearly marked (a red dot), rejoins the river after another hour, but this time do not cross it. Stay on the west side, climb up the slope to an old mill, before dropping steeply down to Pampaneira. By now it will be high time for a break, e. g. in **Casa Julio**, followed by a stroll around this beautiful village. Have a look as the **Plaza Libertad** and the 17th-century church of Santa Cruz. Traditional rugs made in the high-lying Alpujarras can be found in the shops here. Leave the village via the steep Calle Real and follow the **Camino Real** to Bubión. The path is easy to spot as it is part of the long-distance footpath GR7 and marked with a red-and-white bar. The buildings in Bubión are in the traditional style of the region. The *terraos*, the flat-roofs of the simple dwellings, are covered in launa – a clay-like soil – that attracts moisture and seals the roof. Depending on how fit you are, you can take the shorter route back by simply following the road to Capileira, or follow the valley path again to Puente Molino, arriving at the picturesque village that you left 5 –6 hours ago (depending on how fast you walk) from below.

4 CYCLING AMONG THE OLIVES

The gentle hills and extensive olive plantations of the Sierra Subbética are among Andalucía's lesser known stretches of countryside. A bicycle is the perfect means of transport to explore this open area and some of its beautiful villages. The route chosen covers a distance of 48km (30mi) one way and offers 96km (60mi) of traffic-free cycling there and back. Our tip: a leaflet on this stretch can be downloaded from the Vías Verdes website: *www.viasverdes.com/folletos/vv_subbetica_folleto.pdf*.

The **Vía Verde de la Subbética** runs to the north of the Natural Park over a total distance of 56km (35mi). The Vía Verde del Aceite, which extends 55km (34mi) as far as Jaén, joins on at the eastern end. The former station *(estación)* in Luque is a practical place to start. It is right on the N432 and easy to find. If you need to hire a bike, ask the landlord at the pub. However, it is better to come with your own. And off you go! After 8km (5mi) you will reach Zuheros where you can have a short break.

This white village is spectacularly located on a rocky outcrop. Just before reaching the former station, cross the Bailón gorge via an old steel bridge. The intensely green countryside with rock crags and little villages automatically makes you think of a miniature landscape for a model railway. The highest point of the route is reached at km 20. It is not actually really strenuous considering that the difference in altitude between the start and here is only 200m (656ft). But it is still nice to know that it is basically downhill from here. After Doña Mencia and some 5km (3mi), before reaching Cabra, the cycle path goes through a tunnel – and it's 140m (460ft) long without any lighting. Take a break at km 33 where you will find the **Centro de Interpretación del Tren de Aceite** visitor centre with interesting information about the area. You can also get clued up a few miles further on at Lucena station where hand-crafted items are available for sale too. The next few miles pass through the less attractive suburbs of Lucena. But don't worry – it soon becomes green again. You cross several bridges and the endless rows of olive trees in this flat stretch of countryside glide past. After Navas del Selpillar, about 10km (6mi) from Puente Genil, the cycle path suddenly ends.

The return trip from the **Estación de Luque** is 96km (60mi). Those prefering a shorter tour should turn back at the old station in Cabra. That is a return journey of 45km (28mi) and you avoid the area around Lucena.

SPORTS & ACTIVITIES

Andalucía's varied countryside provides all sorts of different possibilities for an active holiday. Golf all year round, skiing in the Sierra Nevada, watersports on both the Atlantic and the Mediterranean, hiking and cycling in the Natural Parks.

The south is well known internationally for its golf courses and for surfing in Tarifa. The densely forested Sierra de Aracena is perfect for hiking. Even for many Spaniards the mountainous Sierra Morena north of Córdoba is unknown territory. The Sierra de Cazorla, Segura y las Villas in the northeast is the largest protected area. Riding, climbing and canyoning are becoming increasingly popular. The actively-minded will enjoy exploring this mountainous area which is home to vultures, eagles and even wolves living in the wild. The desert-like region around Cabo de Gata is also fascinating. Further information can be obtained at local tourist offices.

CLIMBING

Climbing in Andalucía is fashionable. The Garganta del Chorro near Antequera attracts international climbing freaks. There is a challenging area near Tarifa in the Sierra de San Bartolomé and also

Mountainbikers, hikers, surfers and golfers – everyone will always find what they want at any time of the year here in Andalucía

in Grazalema. The climbing school website *www.escuelasdeescalada.com* is useful for orientation but is only available in Spanish.

CYCLING

Cycling in Andalucía is gaining in popularity. The *Vías Verdes*, former railway lines turned into cycle and hiking paths *(see p. 109)*, pass over old bridges and through tunnels. (20 routes at present, information, bike hire and route details under: *www.viasverdes.com*). Organised tours are available, e.g. through *Almería Bike Tours (tel. 9 50 31 73 00 | www.almeria-bike-tours. com)*. See also *Camaleón Sports (near Hotel Costa Conil | Avda. de la Marina | Conil de la Frontera | tel. 6 39 43 14 64 | www.camaleonsports.de/eng_home.htm)*.

DIVING

Diving in the Mediterranean and Atlantic is possible from a number of different places. The undersea world in the INSIDERTIP Marine Natural Park between Caboneras and Cabo de Gata is particularly impressive. Experienced divers are attracted by shipwrecks in the Strait of Gibraltar and the area around Nerja. Local companies include *ISUB (San José | C/ Babor 3 | tel. 9 50 38 00 04 | www.isub-sanjose.com)* in the Natural Park, *Buceo Costa Nerja (Nerja | Playa Burriana | tel. 9 52 52 86 10 | www.nerjadiving.com)* and *Happy Diver's Club (Atalaya Park Hotel | Ctra. de Cádiz, at km 168.5 | Estepona | tel. 9 52 88 36 17 | www.happy-divers-marbella.com)*. For further information contact the *Andalucáin diving association (tel. 9 50 27 06 12 | www.fedas.es/federac/ fed_andaluza.htm)*.

GOLF

There is no other region in Europe where there are so many golf courses so close together than on the Costa del Sol. However other places on the coast and further inland are trying to woo golf-lovers too. There are 137 golf clubs in Andalucía in total, including the most famous of all Spanish courses – the Club Valderrama in Sotogrande. Information on courses and green requirements: *Federación Andaluza de Golf (tel. 9 52 22 55 90 | www.fga.org | www.golfinspain.com)*.

DEHESA MONTENMEDIO

Well-maintained, 18-hole Golf & Country Club course near Vejer de la Frontera, considered one of the most beautiful in Europe. The views from the course are spectacular. *Green fee from 72 euros | Ctra. N340, at km 42.5 | tel. 9 56 45 50 04 | www.montenmediogolf.com*

VALDERRAMA

Since the Ryder Cup was held here in 1997 this course has become world famous. Regardless of your handicap you will enjoy a game here. *Guests admitted daily 12 noon–2pm, register several months in advance | green fee 300 euros | Avda. de Los Cortijos 1 | Sotogrande (near San Roque) | tel. 9 56 79 12 00 | www.valderrama.com*

HIKING

The *Centros de Interpretación* have maps and suggested tours. The paths however are often poorly marked.

SIERRA DE ARACENA

Information about hiking and forest walks available in Aracena in the *Centro de Interpretación del Parque Natural. Closed Mon | Plaza Alta | tel. 9 59 12 88 25*

SIERRA DE GRAZALEMA

Visitor centre in El Bosque (Mon–Fri 10am–2pm, Sat 9am–2pm, 5pm–7pm, Sun 9am–2pm | Avda. de la Diputación 1 | tel. 9 56 72 70 29).
Horizón (C/Corrales Terceros 29 | tel. 9 56 13 23 63 | www.horizonaventura.com) in Grazalema organises interesting hikes.

SIERRA NEVADA

The *Centro de Interpretación del Parque Nacional El Dornajo* has the best information on hiking routes through the National Park *(daily 9.30am–2.30pm, 4.30pm–7.30pm | Ctra. de la Sierra Nevada, at km 23 | tel. 9 58 34 06 25).*

RIDING

Countless stables *(picaderos)* organise rides along the coast, through bull-grazing land and on paths in the parks, for either a few hours or several days. For riding

The Natural and National Parks offer a number of beautiful hill-walking routes

holiday tips see, e.g., *www.equestrian-escapes.com* or *riding-holidays-in-spain.com*

AVENTURA ECUESTRE
Organised rides along Tarifa beach or through Alcornocales Nature Park, as well as across the dunes and full-day hacks. *Hotel Dos Mares | Tarifa | tel. 9 56 23 66 32 | www.aventuraecuestre.com*

RANCHO LA PAZ
Rides and tours lasting several days through the Serranía de Ronda or on beaches on the Atlantic coast. *Torreblanca del Sol | Fuengirola | tel. 9 52 59 02 64 | www.rancho-la-paz.com*

SKIING

The Sierra Nevada is Europe's most southerly skiing area with 118 ski runs and a total of 104km (65mi). At weekends in winter from Dec–April *Pradollano* *(2080m/6824ft)*, easily reached by car, is packed. *Ski pass from 41 euros | www.sierranevada.es*

WINDSURFING & KITESURFING

Tarifa is one of the best places for surfers in Europe. The Strait of Gibraltar acts as a wind tunnel and is perfect for the more experienced wind and kitesurfer. Several surfing centres can be found to the northwest of Tarifa *(www.tarifa.com)* on the N340 and on the beaches towards Punta Paloma, e.g. *Spin Out (Ctra. Cádiz, at km 75.5 | tel. 9 56 23 63 52); Dos Mares (Ctra. Cádiz, at km 79.5 | tel. 9 56 68 40 35)*. Those who prefer a more gentle breeze head for the Mediterranean, e.g. *Roquetas de Mar (www.surfroquetas.com)* on the Costa de Almería. Wave surfers congregate at El Palmar. Good conditions for stand-up paddling can be found in Tarifa, Marbella, Roquetas and El Palmar.

TRAVEL WITH KIDS

Andalucíans love children, especially those they don't know. The tiny ones in particular are always being hugged without parents even batting an eyelid. Travelling with children here is totally problem-free. They are very much part of everyday life in Spain and there is plenty for them to do in Andalucía.

THE WEST

AQUOPOLIS SEVILLA
(137 E4) (*ℳ D4*)
Big water park in the east of the city with lots of attractions. *Early June–early Sept daily 12 noon–7pm, July/Aug 8pm | admission 22 euros, children up to 1.40m (4ft 7in.) tall 16 euros | www.sevilla.aquopolis.es*

COTO DE DOÑANA
(137 D5–6) (*ℳ C5–6*)
Wild horses, boars and deer, waterbirds and fanscinating scenery can all be enjoyed on a 4x4 tour of the national park. *May–mid Sept Mon–Sat 8.30am and 5pm, mid Sept–April Tue–Sun 8.30am and 3pm | 29.50 euros | Centro de Recepción El Acebuche (tel. 9 59 43 04 32 | www.dona-navisitas.es). A boat trip into the Doñana from Sanlúcar de Barrameda is also thrilling: Centro de Visitantes Fábrica de Hielo*

Andalucía is extremely child-friendly –
and children are always taken everywhere,
often staying up until late at night

*(daily 10am, April/May/Oct also 4pm,
June–Sept also 5pm | 17.25 euros | Avda.
Bajo de Guia s/n | tel. 9 56 36 38 13 | www.
visitasdonana.com)*

ISLA MÁGICA (137 E4) (*D4*)
Leisure park on the former Expo site in
Sevilla that relives the time of the con-
quests. *Opening times vary: 11am/12 noon–
7pm/9pm/11pm/midnight | admission*

*29 euros, children (5–12) 21 euros | www.
islamagica.es*

MUELLE DE LAS CARABELAS
(136 B4) (*B5*)
True-to-original replicas of the three ships
with which Columbus and his crew set sail
in 1492, in La Rábida at the mouth of the
Río Tinto. *June–Sept Tue–Fri 10am–2pm,
5pm–9pm, Sat/Sun 11am–8pm, Oct–May*

Tue–Sun 10am–7pm | admission 3.55 euros, families with children 7.45 euros

INSIDER TIP PARQUE MINERO DE RÍO TINTO (136 C3) (*⌕ C3*)

Metal ore has been mined on the Río Tinto in Huelva province for thousands of year. The area's mining history and a replica of a Roman mine are on display in a museum in Minas de Riotinto (*daily 10.30am–3pm, 4pm–7pm, Aug 8pm |*

RESERVA NATURAL EL CASTILLO DE LAS GUARDAS (137 D3) (*⌕ C3*)

Safari park, 58km (36mi) northwest of Sevilla. A 10km (6mi)-circular route leads through an enclosure with 1000 animals, incl. giraffes, rhinos and elephants, either in your own car or on a small train. *Daily 10.30am–5.30pm (summer 6.30pm) | admission 22.50, children (up to 12) 16.50 euros | Castillo de las Guardas | www. lareservadelcastillodelasguardas.com*

Perfect for children of any age – Andalucía's beautiful beaches

admission: museum incl. a trip on the diesel train 20 euros, children 18 euros | Plaza Ernest Lluch). The spectacular *Corta Atalaya*, the largest open-cast mine in Europe, can also be visited. Other attractions include a ride on Spain's oldest steam locomotive still in operation (*Nov–April every first Sun). Reservations tel. 9 59 59 00 25 | www.parqueminiderodriotinto. com*

THE EAST

ACUARIO ALMUÑÉCAR ●
(145 E5) (*⌕ K6*)

Maritime aquarium with some 200 species with viewing tunnel. *Daily 10.30am–10pm or 10am–6.30pm depending on season | admission 12 euros, children (up to 12) 9 euros | Plaza Kuwait | www.acuario almunecar.es*

AQUA TROPIC (145 E5) (⚇ K6)
Water park on Almuñécar beach. *Mid June–Sept daily 11am–7pm | admission 17 euros, Junior (12–15) 16 euros, children (4–11) 13 euros, Sun 1 euro surcharge | Paseo Marítimo, Playa de Velilla | www.aqua-tropic.com*

PARQUE DE LAS CIENCIAS ●
(145 E3) (⚇ K5)
This science park is the most visited museum in Andalucía. Everyone is welcome to do their own experiments. Special area for 3–7 year-olds. *Tue–Sat 10am–7pm, Sun 10am–3pm | admission 6.50 euros, children 5.50 euros, Planetarium 2.50 euros, children 2 euros | Avda. del Mediterráneo s/n | Granada | www.parqueciencias.com*

PARQUE ORNITOLÓGICO LORO SEXI
(145 E5) (⚇ K6)
Beautifully laid out ornithological park with 200 species of tropical bird. *Daily June–mid Sept 10.30am–2pm, 5pm–9pm, April–May 10.30am–2pm, 3pm–6.30pm, mid Sept–March 10.30am–2pm, 3pm–6pm | admission 5 euros, children 3 euros | www.lorosexi.com*

SIERRA NEVADA (145 E–F4) (⚇ K5)
Summer toboggan run 4.50 euros per ride. In winter: ice-skating 7 euros/hr., mini ski, bike ski 17 euros/hr. In resort of the same name. www.sierranevada.es

THE SOUTH

AQUALAND (142 B4) (⚇ D7)
June–Sept daily 11am–6pm, July, Aug 7pm | El Puerto de Santa María, Ctra. NIV, at km 646 | admission 21 euros, children (up to 12) 16 euros | www.aqualand.es

CROCODILOS PARK (144 B6) (⚇ G7)
400 crocs, from the freshly hatched to up to others 4m (13ft) long. *Daily 10am–early evening | admission 13 euros, children (up to 12) 10 euros | Torremolinos | C/ Cuba 14 | www.cocodrilospark.com*

PARQUE ACUÁTICO MIJAS
(144 B6) (⚇ G7)
Best water park, near Fuengirola. *May daily 10.30am–5.30pm, June and Sept daily 10am–6pm, July/Aug daily 10am–7pm | admission 20 euros, children (4–12) 15 euros | Ctra. N 340, km 209 | www.aquamijas.com*

SEA LIFE BENALMÁDENA
(144 B6) (⚇ H7)
Lovely underwater zoo, esp. suitable for small children who will love the seahorses. *Daily 10am–8pm | admission 16.25 euros, children (4–12) 14 euros | Puerto Deportivo Benalmádena | www.sealife.es*

SELWO AVENTURA
(143 E4) (⚇ F7)
Adventure park, a colourful mixture of zoo and fair. Children love it. *Feb–April, Sept–Nov daily 10am–6pm, May/June 10am–7pm, July/Aug 10am–8pm | admission 24.50 euros, children (3–7) 17 euros | Autovía Costa del Sol, km 162,5 | www.selwo.es*

SELWO MARINA (144 B6) (⚇ H7)
Water park on the Costa del Sol with a delphin show. *Feb–Nov daily 10am–6pm (June and Sept 9pm, July/Aug midnight) | admission 19 euros, children (3–9) 15 euros | Parque de la Paloma Benalmádena | www.selwomarina.es*

WHALE WATCHING
(142 C6) (⚇ E8)
The Strait of Gibraltar is not only an important waterway for ships but also for delphins and whales. Whale Watch runs tours from Tarifa *(www.whalewatchtarifa.net)* as does firmm *(www.firmm.org)*. *Price approx. 30 euros, children 20 euros*

FESTIVALS & EVENTS

The most famous festivals in Andalucía are religious ones. The Semana Santa and the pilgrimage to El Rocío are powerful expressions of devoutness. And who can differentiate between spontaneous emotional expression and deep-rooted religious feeling? But more than praising the Virgin Mary or the Son of God the Andalucíans like celebrating life itself. Every festival is a wonderful opportunity to dig out those beautiful costumes from the wardrobe, have your hair done (or grease it back with gel) and polish those shoes until you can see your face in them.

PUBLIC HOLIDAYS

1 Jan *Año Nuevo*, **6 Jan** *Reyes* (Epiphany), **28 Feb** *Día de Andalucía*, **Jueves Santo** (Maundy Thursday), **Viernes Santo** (Good Friday), **1 May** *Día del Trabajo* (Labour Day), **15 Aug** *Asunción* (Assumption), **12 Oct** *Día de la Hispanidad* (Columbus' discovery of America), **1 Nov** *Todos los Santos* (All Saints), **6 Dez** *Día de la Constitución* (Constitution Day), **8 Dec** *Inmaculada Concepción* (Feast of the Immaculate Conception), **25 Dec** *Navidad* (Christmas)

FESTIVALS AND EVENTS

FEBRUARY

▶ *Carnival of Cádiz* – lasts until the Sunday after Ash Wednesday. *www.carnavaldecadiz.com*

▶ ★ *Festival de Jerez* – 2-week long flamenco festival with the very best artists from the end of Feb/early March. *www.festivaldejerez.es*

MARCH/APRIL

▶ ★ *Semana Santa* (Holy Week) – celebrated in Andalucía with magnificent processions, the most famous and spectacular being in Sevilla. Those in Granada, Córdoba, Málaga, ● Úbeda and Jaén are equally worth seeing. The climax is the night before Good Friday

▶ ★ *Feria de Abril* – the 7-day April Market in Sevilla, 8 days after Easter, is the biggest public festival in Andalucía when the streets are full of horses and carriages, elegant riders and women in local costume

▶ *Festival de Cine Español de Málaga* – the largest Spanish film festival. *www.festivaldemalaga.com*

Regardless of whether a festival is religious or secular the Andalucíans enjoy celebrating everything – especially themselves

MAY

▶ *Spanish Grand Prix* – motorbike race in Jerez. *www.circuitodejerez.com*

▶ *Cruces de Mayo* – brightly decorated crosses are displayed in many towns during the first week in May

▶ *Feria del Caballo* – the horse market in Jerez is the city's biggest festival

▶ INSIDER TIP *Festival de los Patios Cordobeses* – competition for Córdoba's most beautiful courtyard

WHITSUN

▶ ⭐ *Pilgrimage to El Rocío* – by hundreds of thousands of pilgrims, some on horseback, to the 'Virgin of the Dew' in El Rocío

END JUNE/EARLY JULY

▶ *Fiesta de San Juan – 24 June* – midsummer's night with firework display

▶ *Festival Internacional de Música y Danza de Granada* – important festival of classical and contemporary music and ballet in Granada. *www.granadafestival.org*

▶ *Festival de la Cueva* – ballet, opera and concerts at the end of July in the caves in Nerja. *www.cuevadenerja.es*

AUGUST

▶ INSIDER TIP *Carreras de Caballo de Sanlúcar de Barrameda* – horse racing on the sandy banks of the Guadalquivir. *www.carrerassanlucar.es*

EARLY SEPTEMBER

▶ *Feria de Pedro Romero* – bullfighting festival in Ronda incl. the 'Corrida Goyesca' – as performed in Goya's day. *www.turismoderonda.es*

NOVEMBER

▶ *Festival de Jazz de Granada* – one of the most important of its kind in Europe. *www.jazzgranada.es*

LINKS, BLOGS, APPS & MORE

LINKS

▶ www.andalucia.org/en Everything you ever wanted to know about holidaying in Andalucía, with news, tips, planning tips, destinations, an events calendar, interactive maps. etc.

▶ www.iberianature.com/directory/adventure-sports-and-outdoor-activities-in-spain/hiking-in-spain/hiking-in-andalucia/ A useful guide to hikes in the mountains and parks in western Andalucía, whether with a group or on your own

▶ www.andalucia.com/province/home.htm With all sorts of information, also for those planning to settle in the region

BLOGS

▶ blog.andalucia.com You name it, it's on a blog here. Anything vaguely related to the Andalucían experience is commented on here for all to read

▶ andaluciablog.blogspot.com News in English about all things Andalucían as well as useful tips

▶ www.expat-blog.com Enter 'Andalusia' and off you go! Ideal for anyone wanting to work, live or move to Andalucía. Or simply for those wanting to find out about life in the far south. Blogs written by expats living in the region

VIDEOS & STREAMS

▶ www.youtube.com/watch?v=juJ3vkLDKaw Flamenco dancing in the streets of Sevilla showing the spontaneity and pure pleasure of dancing. With links to all sorts of related videos

▶ uk.video.search.yahoo.com/search/video?p=andalucia+video+alhambra A wide selection of videos giving you an idea of the magnificence of the Alhambra in Granada

Regardless of whether you are still preparing your trip or already in Andalucía: these addresses will provide you with more information, videos and networks to make your holiday even more enjoyable

VIDEOS & STREAMS

▶ uk.video.search.yahoo.com/search/video?p=andalucia+video+national+parks The same applies to this site where you are taken on a trip round some of the National and Natural Parks in Andalucía

▶ www.youtube.com/watch?v=g-D7WHGWLUs An interesting report on the pilgrimage in El Rocío. Although only in Spanish it gives a good impression of the devout procession

APPS

▶ www.7thspace.com/app-store/app-details/353427/andalucia.html A constantly-updated travel planner for Andalucía written by a resident of Spain

▶ Beaches of Costa del Sol This app lists all the beaches on the Costa del Sol, with photos and useful information for visitors

▶ Diarios de España If you can speak Spanish, this app keeps you up-to-date on what is going on in the country with a summary of the news from the major national papers such as El País, ABC, Diario de Sevilla, etc.

▶ HRS Hotelportal Find out if rooms are still available and check the up-to-the-minute prices on this well-known hotel portal. With in-built GPS for finding hotels nearby. Free download for Apple und Android

NETWORK

▶ twitter.com/sevillaciudad Everything that's going on in Andalucía's capital can be found here in the typical brief twitter manner in English and Spanish

▶ www.facebook.com/costadelsolspain With some 8000 Costa del Sol fans who are just dying to show you their holidy snaps and anything that could interest sun-worshippers on the coast

▶ www.facebook.com/andalusia Typical site for Andalucía fans

▶ twitter.com/viveandalucia With all sorts of details about sports events, concerts, news and culture. Many things are shown in real-time via the Andalucía ticker in Spanish

TRAVEL TIPS

ARRIVAL

✈ The most important airport in Andalucía is Málaga (abbreviation: AGP). It is just 10km (6¼mi) from the city centre. This is where holiday-makers land who are staying on the Costa del Sol or Costa Tropical. The best infrastructure for individual travellers can also be found here with good bus and train connections as well as the usual car hire companies. easyJet, bmibaby and Ryanair, as well as Iberia and British Airways depart from various British airports for Málaga and Almería. Almería (LEI, 10km/6¼mi from the city centre) is well located for the east of Andalucía. Granada airport (GRX, 23km/14mi from the city centre) is an option for connecting flights to and from Madrid or Barcelona. Jerez de la Frontera (XRY, 12km/7½mi from the city centre) is perfect for those aiming for the west Costa del Sol and east Costa de la Luz. Iberia and Ryanair fly here as well as to Sevilla

(SVQ, 12km/7½mi from the city centre). Alternatives are Madrid (approx. 300km/186mi from north Andalucía) or Faro in Portugal (approx. 70km/44mi from west Andalucía). From Madrid take the AVE (high-speed train) which will get you to Sevilla or Córdoba in 2½ hrs. (return fare from around 160 euros). The Spanish airport portal is *www.aena.es*. For up-to-date information consult the websites of the various airlines.

🚗 Andalucía is a long way from the UK. Allow 2½–3 days to get to Spain by car. The distances from London to Almería is 2300km (1500mi). The most direct route is via Paris, Marseille and Barcelona. Alternatively take the ferry from Portsmouth or Plymouth to Santander or Bilbao and drive down across the country. Route planners are available on the Internet and help calculate the cost of the trip as they include toll fees for motorways in France and Spain.

🚆 The journey by train can take up to 30 hrs. and involves several changes. The cost is generally higher than a plane ticket. For more information see: *www.renfe.com* and *www.seat61.com*

CAMPING

Information on the more than 100 campsites in Andalucía can be obtained from the *Federación Andaluza de Campings (www.andaluciacampings.com)* or under *www.campingsonline.com*.

CAR HIRE

Depending on the season and model, a

RESPONSIBLE TRAVEL

It doesn't take a lot to be environmentally friendly whilst travelling. Don't just think about your carbon footprint whilst flying to and from your holiday destination but also about how you can protect nature and culture abroad. As a tourist it is especially important to respect nature, look out for local products, cycle instead of driving, save water and much more. If you would like to find out more about eco-tourism please visit: *www.ecotourism.org*

hire car costs anything from 25 euros a day. *Nizacars (tel. 9 52 23 61 79 | www.nizacars. es)* and *Prima Rent a Car (tel. 9 52 31 09 75 | www.rentacarprima.com)* can be found in most resorts. It is however advisable to book a car before leaving which avoids any insurance and 'full tank of petrol' problems – beware of unclear wording in this respect when hiring locally.

CONSULATES & EMBASSIES

BRITISH CONSULATE
Edificio Eurocom | Calle Mauriccio Moro Pareto 2 | 29006 Málaga | tel. 9 02 10 93 56 | www.ukinspain.fco.gov.uk

CONSULATE OF THE UNITED STATES OF AMERICA
Edificio Lucio 1°-C | Avenida Juan Gómez Juanito 8 | 29640 Fuengirola | tel. 9 52 47 48 91 | madrid.usembassy.gov

CONSULATE OF CANADA
Plaza de la Malagueta 2, 1° | 29016 Málaga | tel. 9 52 22 33 46 | www.canada international.gc.ca

CUSTOMS

For EU citizens the following duty free al-lowances apply (import and export): for own consumption 800 cigarettes, 400 cigarillos, 200 cigars, 1kg tobacco, 20L aperitif, 90L wine (with a maximum amount of 60L sparkling wine) and 110L beer.

Travellers to the US who are residents of the country do not have to pay duty on articles purchased overseas up to the value of $800, but there are limits on the amount of alcoholic beverages and to-

BUDGETING

Taxi	£1/$1.60	per kilometer
Coffee	£1.25/$2	for a café solo
Dining	£5/$8	for a bowl of gazpacho
Wine	£2.50/$4	for a glass of wine
Petrol	£1.25/$2	for 1 litre (super)
Sunbed	£7.50/$12	rental a day

bacco products. For the regulations for international travel for US residents please see *www.cbp.gov*

DRIVING

The Andalucían road network has been expanded. Provincial capitals are all linked by motorways and the few gaps are being filled in bit by bit. Tolls are payable on only a few motorways in Andalucía – these are marked 'AP' *(autopista de peaje)*. The main roads (with numbers beginning with an 'N' or 'A') are virtually all in good condition (the 'A' stands for Andalucía not *autopista*). The speed limit in built-up areas is 50 km/h (30 mph), on country roads 90 km/h (55 mph) and 120 km/h (75mph) on motorways. The legal drink-driving limit is a blood alcohol level of 0.5mg per ml. Seatbelts must be worn; telephoning while driving is only allowed with a hands-free headset; the engine, lights and electrical appliances must all be turned off when fuelling. Drivers must

Street café in Granada

HEALTH

If you need a doctor quickly ask for the nearest hospital with an A&E *(urgencia)*. Reckon with a long wait. The Spanish health system is medically up-to-date but generally overburdened. If you have a European Health Insurance Card (EHIC) you will no longer need the formula E111. This will entitle you to free treatment in state hospitals and from doctors belonging to the 'Servicio Andaluz de Salud' (SAS). Payment for treatment at private practices or clinics has to be done on the spot. Look into travel health insurance before leaving.

IMMIGRATION

You will need a valid passport – even though it is no longer checked on immigration from Schengen countries – and should have it on you at all times in the case of police checks (for motorists), when notifying a theft etc. Tourists from America, Canada and Australia do not need a visa for stays under 90 days. Border controls in Gibraltar may take some time.

INFORMATION

SPANISH TOURIST OFFICE TURESPAÑA
– *64 North Row| W1K 7DE, London | tel. 020 7317 2011 | www.spain.info*
– *845 North Michigan Av, Suite 915-E | Chicago IL 60611| tel. 312 642 1992| www. spain.info/en_US*
– *20 East 42nd Street, Suite 5300 | New York NY 10165-0039| tel. 216 265 8822| www.spain.info/en_US*

have high visibility vests with them in the case of a breakdown. Children under 3 must be strapped into a suitable childr seats. EU citizens must have their driving licence with them as well as a certificate of insurance and proof of payment or a green insurance card. Help in the case of a breakdown is available from the automobile club RACE, *tel. 9 02 30 05 05*.

EMERGENCY SERVICES

Central emergency no. for police, fire brigade and other emegency services: *tel. 112*.

INTERNET CAFÉS & WI-FI

Wi-Fi is now widely available in many hotels, cafés and in official buildings. Wi-Fi is provided in Spain by the Wireless

Ethernet Compatibility Alliance. Almost every tourist resort has an Internet café. And public libraries also usually have Internet access.

MONEY & PRICES

Andalucía is still a little cheaper than England. Money can be obtained from cash dispensers everywhere using an EC card. Credit cards are accepted in hotels, shops and better restaurants, but not necessarily in taxis or hostels/guesthouses. Always ask in advance. Banks are generally open *Mon–Fri 8am–2.30pm*.

OPENING HOURS

The opening hours in this guidebook have been carefully researched. Having said this, there is nothing in Spain that changes as quickly as the days and times a tourist attraction is open. Tourist information offices should know the up-to-date times. Restaurants also frequently change their opening times – it is always best to ring in advance.

PETS

Generally speaking, a certificate from a vet or a pet passport must always accompany an animal. Dogs and cats have to be inoculated against rabies and marked with a tattoo or microchip. Not all places to stay accept animals by any means.

PHONE & MOBILE PHONE

The international code for calling Spain from abroad is *+34* followed by the complete number. To call other countries, dial the country code (UK *+44*, US *+1*, Ireland *+353*), and then the telephone number without *0*. Even for local calls in Spain you must always dial the 9-digit number.

Olives in Jaén

CURRENCY CONVERTER

£	€	€	£
1	1.20	1	0.85
3	3.60	3	2.55
5	6	5	4.25
13	15.60	13	11
40	48	40	34
75	90	75	64
120	144	120	100
250	300	250	210
500	600	500	425

$	€	€	$
1	0.75	1	1.30
3	2.30	3	3.90
5	3.80	5	6.50
13	10	13	17
40	30	40	50
75	55	75	97
120	90	120	155
250	185	250	325
500	370	500	650

For current exchange rates see www.xe.com

Telefónica phone boxes take coins and phone cards. At present, the fee for mobile calls to other European countries must not exceed 35 cents/min.; incoming calls cost a max. 10 cents. A prepaid SIM card in Spain (with Orange, for example) costs 5 euros and every national call costs .09 cents a minute. Mailboxes can be expensive. It is advisable to disable this function before leaving home.

POST

Post offices *(oficinas de correos)* are generally open *Mon–Fri 8.30am–2.30pm* and *Sat 9.30am–1pm (www.correos.es)*. Stamps can be bought at tobacconists too *(estancos)*. A standard letter or postcard within Europe costs 75 cents at present.

PUBLIC TRANSPORT

The Spanish railway network is not very extensive. There is however a good high-speed rail link (AVE) between Madrid via Córdoba to Sevilla and from Madrid to Málaga. Travelling by train on these routes can be highly recommended. Enjoy the scenery and save the hastle of looking for somewhere to park. If you want to travel to other places in Andalucía by train you will need some patience. The state-run railway is called RENFE. For information and reservations: *tel. 9 02 32 03 20* |

WEATHER IN MÁLAGA

	Jan	Feb	March	April	May	June	July	Aug	Sept	Oct	Nov	Dec
Daytime temperatures in °C/°F	16/61	17/63	18/64	21/70	23/73	27/81	29/84	29/84	27/81	23/73	19/66	17/63
Nighttime temperatures in °C/°F	8/46	9/48	11/52	13/55	16/61	19/66	21/70	22/72	20/68	16/61	12/54	9/48
Sunshine hours/day	6	6	6	8	10	11	11	11	9	7	6	5
Precipitation days/month	5	5	6	3	2	1	0	0	2	4	6	5
Water temperatures in °C/°F	15/59	14/57	14/57	15/59	17/63	18/64	21/70	22/72	21/70	19/66	17/63	16/61

www.renfe.es or *Ibero Tours (tel. 0211 8 64 15 20 | www.ibero.com)*. Long-distance coaches run frequently and are a good alternative. Enquire at the tourist information office for the nearest bus station *(estación de autobuses)*. Buses and trains are comparatively cheap.

SMOKING

Prohibido fumar, 'No smoking', is the notice you will see all over Spain since January 2011. And the anti-smoking laws have since been tightened and smoking is now banned in restaurants, bars, pubs and discos, and also in public buildings such as airports, and not even smoking areas are permitted in the workplace nor in pubs and restaurants.

TIME

Andalucía is one hour ahead of Greenwich Mean Time and six hours ahead of US Eastern Time.

TIPS

When the waiter/waitress brings you your change on a plate, add a few coins – the going rate is up to 10%. Taxi fares should be rounded up. In hotels, chambermaids/roomboys are given 1–2 euros.

TOBACCONISTS

Stamps and phone cards can be bought at state-licenced tobacconists – *estancos* (a brown 'T' on a yellow background). Cigarettes are generally slightly cheaper here than from machines.

WEATHER, WHEN TO GO

Spring and autumn are the most pleasant times of year in Andalucía. In July/Aug you will have to deal with searing heat; the nights however are balmy. The Spanish school holidays are from July–Sept as well as between Christmas and 6 Jan and during Semana Santa. It is very difficult finding accommodation at short notice at this time. Winters are cool and sometimes wet but not cold and the main sites not crowded.

YOUTH HOSTELS

Information on the 21 youth hostels in Andalucía is available under: *tel. 9 02 51 00 00* and *www.inturjoven.com*.

The legacy of the Romans: Baelo Claudia near Bolonia

USEFUL PHRASES SPANISH

PRONUNCIATION

c	before 'e' and 'i' like 'th' in 'thin'
ch	as in English
g	before 'e' and 'i' like the 'ch' in Scottish 'loch'
gue, gui	like 'get', 'give'
que, qui	the 'u' is not spoken, i.e. 'ke', 'ki'
j	always like the 'ch' in Scottish 'loch'
ll	like 'lli' in 'million'; some speak it like 'y' in 'yet'
ñ	'nj'
z	like 'th' in 'thin'

IN BRIEF

Yes/No/Maybe	sí/no/quizás
Please/Thank you	por favor/gracias
Hello!/Goodbye!/See you	¡Hola!/¡Adiós!/¡Hasta luego!
Good morning!/afternoon!/evening!/night!	¡Buenos días!/¡Buenos días!/¡Buenas tardes!/¡Buenas noches!
Excuse me, please!	¡Perdona!/¡Perdone!
May I ...?/Pardon?	¿Puedo ...?/¿Cómo dice?
My name is ...	Me llamo ...
What's your name?	¿Cómo se llama usted?/¿Cómo te llamas?
I'm from ...	Soy de ...
I would like to .../Have you got ...?	Querría .../¿Tiene usted ...?
How much is ...?	¿Cuánto cuesta ...?
I (don't) like that	Esto (no) me gusta.
good/bad/broken/doesn't work	bien/mal/roto/no funciona
too much/much/little/all/nothing	demasiado/mucho/poco/todo/nada
Help!/Attention!/Caution!	¡Socorro!/¡Atención!/¡Cuidado!
ambulance/police/fire brigade	ambulancia/policía/bomberos
May I take a photo here	¿Podría fotografiar aquí?

DATE & TIME

Monday/Tuesday/Wednesday	lunes/martes/miércoles
Thursday/Friday/Saturday	jueves/viernes/sábado
Sunday/working day/holiday	domingo/laborable/festivo
today/tomorrow/yesterday	hoy/mañana/ayer

¿Hablas español?

"Do you speak Spanish?" This guide will help you to say the basic words and phrases in Spanish.

hour/minute/second/moment	hora/minuto/segundo/momento
day/night/week/month/year	día/noche/semana/mes/año
now/immediately/before/after	ahora/enseguida/antes/después
What time is it?	¿Qué hora es?
It's three o'clock/It's half past three	Son las tres/Son las tres y media
a quarter to four/a quarter past four	cuatro menos cuarto/ cuatro y cuarto

TRAVEL

open/closed/opening times	abierto/cerrado/horario
entrance / exit	entrada/acceso salida
departure/arrival	salida/llegada
toilets/ladies/gentlemen	aseos/señoras/caballeros
free/occupied	libre/ocupado
(not) drinking water	agua (no) potable
Where is ...?/Where are ...?	¿Dónde está ...? /¿Dónde están ...?
left/right	izquierda/derecha
straight ahead/back	recto/atrás
close/far	cerca/lejos
traffic lights/corner/crossing	semáforo/esquina/cruce
bus/tram/U-underground/	autobús/tranvía/metro/
taxi/cab	taxi
bus stop/cab stand	parada/parada de taxis
parking lot/parking garage	parking/garaje
street map/map	plano de la ciudad/mapa
train station/harbour/airport	estación/puerto/aeropuerto
ferry/quay	transbordador/muelle
schedule/ticket/supplement	horario/billete/suplemento
single/return	sencillo/ida y vuelta
train/track/platform	tren/vía/andén
delay/strike	retraso/huelga
I would like to rent ...	Querría ... alquilar
a car/a bicycle/a boat	un coche/una bicicleta/un barco
petrol/gas station	gasolinera
petrol/gas / diesel	gasolina/diesel
breakdown/repair shop	avería/taller

FOOD & DRINK

Could you please book a table for tonight for four?	Resérvenos, por favor, una mesa para cuatro personas para hoy por la noche.
on the terrace/by the window	en la terraza/junto a la ventana

The menu, please/	¡El menú, por favor!
Could I please have ...?	¿Podría traerme ... por favor?
bottle/carafe/glass	botella/jarra/vaso
knife/fork/spoon	cuchillo/tenedor/cuchara
salt/pepper/sugar	sal/pimienta/azúcar
vinegar/oil/milk/cream/lemon	vinagre/aceite/leche/limón
cold/too salty/not cooked	frío/demasiado salado/sin hacer
with/without ice/sparkling	con/sin hielo/gas
vegetarian/allergy	vegetariano/vegetariana/alergía
May I have the bill, please?	Querría pagar, por favor.
bill/receipt/tip	cuenta/recibo/propina

SHOPPING

pharmacy/chemist	farmacia/droguería
baker/market	panadería/mercado
butcher/fishmonger	carnicería/pescadería
shopping centre/department store	centro comercial/grandes almacenes
shop/supermarket/kiosk	tienda/supermercado/quiosco
100 grammes/1 kilo	cien gramos/un kilo
expensive/cheap/price/more/less	caro/barato/precio/más/menos
organically grown	de cultivo ecológico

ACCOMMODATION

I have booked a room	He reservado una habitación.
Do you have any ... left?	¿Tiene todavía ...?
single room/double room	habitación individual/habitación doble
breakfast/half board/	desayuno/media pensión/
full board (American plan)	pensión completa
at the front/seafront/garden view	hacia delante/hacia el mar/hacia el jardín
shower/sit-down bath	ducha/baño
balcony/terrace	balcón/terraza
key/room card	llave/tarjeta
luggage/suitcase/bag	equipaje/maleta/bolso
swimming pool/spa/sauna	piscina/spa/sauna
soap/toilet paper/nappy (diaper)	jabón/papel higiénico/pañal
cot/high chair/nappy changing	cuna/trona/cambiar los pañales
deposit	anticipo/caución

BANKS, MONEY & CREDIT CARDS

bank/ATM/	banco/cajero automático/
pin code	número secreto
cash/credit card	en efectivo/tarjeta de crédito
bill/coin/change	billete/moneda/cambio

USEFUL PHRASES

HEALTH

doctor/dentist/paediatrician	médico/dentista/pediatra
hospital/emergency clinic	hospital/urgencias
fever/pain/inflamed/injured	fiebre/dolor/inflamado/herido
diarrhoea/nausea/sunburn	diarrea/náusea/quemadura de sol
plaster/bandage/ointment/cream	tirita/vendaje/pomada/crema
pain reliever/tablet/suppository	calmante/comprimido/supositorio

POST, TELECOMMUNICATIONS & MEDIA

stamp/letter/postcard	sello/carta/postal
I need a landline phone card/	Necesito una tarjeta telefónica/
I'm looking for a prepaid card for my mobile	Busco una tarjeta prepago para mi móvil
Where can I find internet access?	¿Dónde encuentro un acceso a internet?
dial/connection/engaged	marcar/conexión/ocupado
socket/adapter/charger	enchufe/adaptador/cargador
computer/battery/ rechargeable battery	ordenador/batería/ batería recargable
e-mail address/at sign (@)	(dirección de) correo electrónico/arroba
internet address (URL)	dirección de internet
internet connection/wifi	conexión a internet/wifi
e-mail/file/print	archivo/imprimir

LEISURE, SPORTS & BEACH

beach/sunshade/lounger	playa/sombrilla/tumbona
low tide/high tide/current	marea baja/marea alta/corriente

NUMBERS

0	cero	14	catorce
1	un, uno, una	15	quince
2	dos	16	dieciséis
3	tres	17	diecisiete
4	cuatro	18	dieciocho
5	cinco	19	diecinueve
6	seis	20	veinte
7	siete	100	cien, ciento
8	ocho	200	doscientos, doscientas
9	nueve	1000	mil
10	diez	2000	dos mil
11	once	10000	diez mil
12	doce	1/2	medio
13	trece	1/4	un cuarto

NOTES

FOR YOUR NEXT HOLIDAY ...

MARCO POLO TRAVEL GUIDES

ALGARVE
AMSTERDAM
ANDALUCÍA
ATHENS
AUSTRALIA
AUSTRIA
BANGKOK
BARCELONA
BERLIN
BRAZIL
BRUGES, GHENT &
  ANTWERP
BRUSSELS
BUDAPEST
BULGARIA
CALIFORNIA
CAMBODIA
CANADA EAST
CANADA WEST
  ROCKIES
CAPE TOWN
  WINE LANDS,
  GARDEN ROUTE
CAPE VERDE
CHANNEL ISLANDS
CHICAGO
  & THE LAKES
CHINA
COLOGNE
COPENHAGEN
CORFU
COSTA BLANCA
  VALENCIA
COSTA BRAVA
  BARCELONA
COSTA DEL SOL
  GRANADA
CRETE
CUBA
CYPRUS
  NORTH AND
  SOUTH
DRESDEN
DUBAI
DUBLIN
DUBROVNIK &
  DALMATIAN COAST
EDINBURGH

EGYPT
EGYPT'S RED
  SEA RESORTS
FINLAND
FLORENCE
FLORIDA
FRENCH ATLANTIC
  COAST
FRENCH RIVIERA
  NICE, CANNES &
  MONACO
FUERTEVENTURA
GRAN CANARIA
GREECE
HAMBURG
HONG KONG
  MACAU
ICELAND
INDIA
INDIA SOUTH
  GOA & KERALA
IRELAND
ISRAEL
ISTANBUL
ITALY
JORDAN
KOS
KRAKOW
LAKE GARDA

LANZAROTE
LAS VEGAS
LISBON
LONDON
LOS ANGELES
MADEIRA
  PORTO SANTO
MADRID
MALLORCA
MALTA
  GOZO
MAURITIUS
MENORCA
MILAN
MONTENEGRO
MOROCCO
MUNICH
NAPLES &
  THE AMALFI COAST
NEW YORK
NEW ZEALAND
NORWAY
OSLO
PARIS
PHUKET
PORTUGAL
PRAGUE

RHODES
ROME
SAN FRANCISCO
SARDINIA
SCOTLAND
SEYCHELLES
SHANGHAI
SICILY
SINGAPORE
SOUTH AFRICA
STOCKHOLM
SWITZERLAND
TENERIFE
THAILAND
TURKEY
TURKEY
  SOUTH COAST
TUSCANY
UNITED ARAB
  EMIRATES
USA SOUTHWEST
VENICE
VIENNA
VIETNAM
ZÁKYNTHOS

MARCO ◉ POLO
With STREET ATLAS & PULL-OUT MAP
FRENCH RIVIERA
NICE, CANNES & MONACO
SPECTACULAR GRAND CANYON DU VERDON
Breath-taking scenery that takes some beating
SNIFFING THE AIR
The perfume manufacturers of Grasse
Insider Tips

MARCO ◉ POLO
EW YORK
WS, WILD FLOWERS AND SKYSCRAPERS
the High Line in Chelsea
ON CLOUD NINE
or at 230 Fifth Street
Insider Tips

MARCO ◉ POLO
ROAD ATLAS & PULL-OUT MAP
AKE GARDA
BALDO WITH MOUNTAIN BIKE
Macasine blasts bikes top
SSES " IN SALÒ
colate "Bucetto"
Insider Tips

MARCO ◉ POLO
With ROAD ATLAS & PULL-OUT MAP
ALLORCA
AN FLAIR IN THE MEDITERRANEAN
Mallorca's most beautiful beach
N" CROWD MEET
rtela in Deià
Insider Tips

MARCO ◉ POLO
With STREET ATLAS & PULL-OUT MAP
BERLIN
A STUNNING ISLAND JUST FOR ART
Showcasing treasures from around the world
Y COOL AT NIGHT
club scene sets the trend
Insider Tips

- PACKED WITH INSIDER TIPS
- BEST WALKS AND TOURS
- FULL-COLOUR PULL-OUT MAP
  AND STREET ATLAS

ROAD ATLAS

The green line ▬▬ indicates the Trips & Tours (p. 104–109)
The blue line ▬▬ indicates The perfect route (p. 30–31)

All tours are also marked on the pull-out map

Photo: Puente Romano, Córdoba

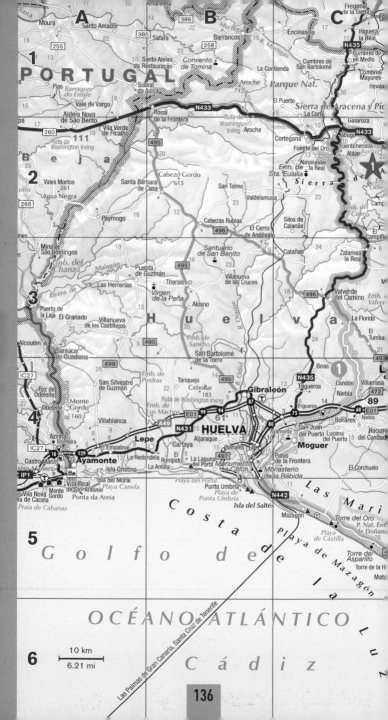

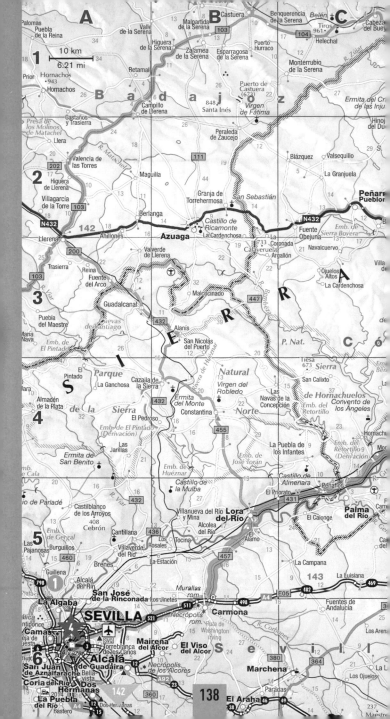

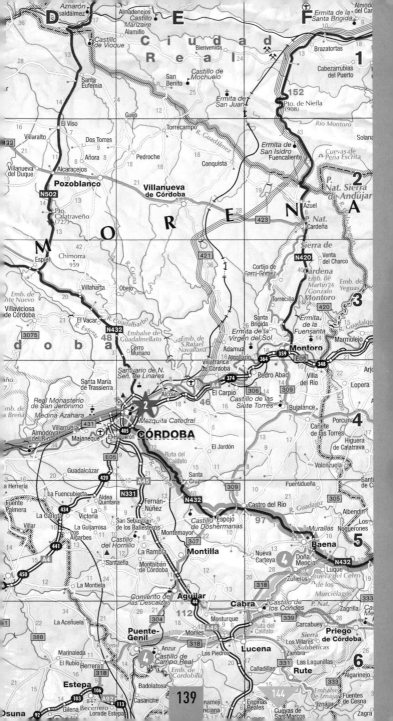

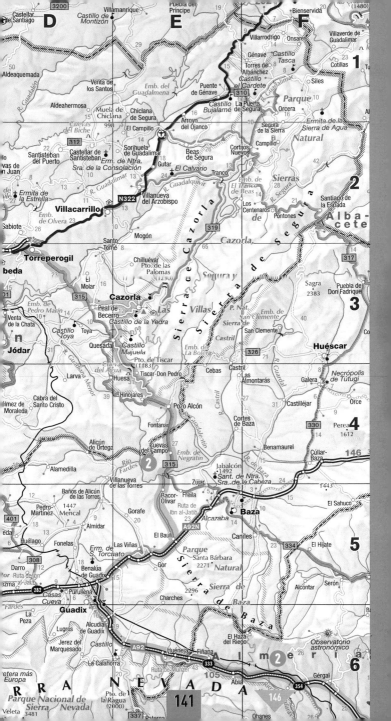

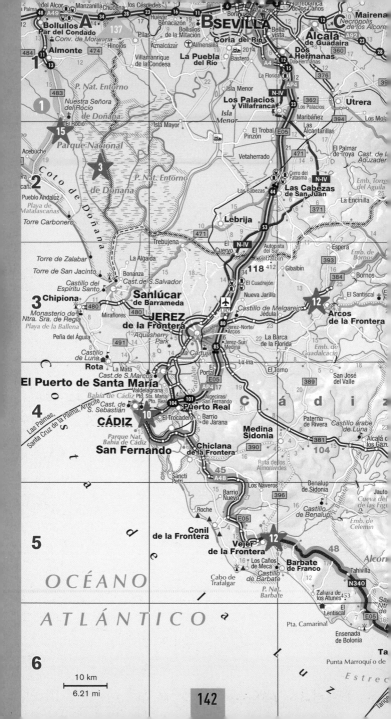

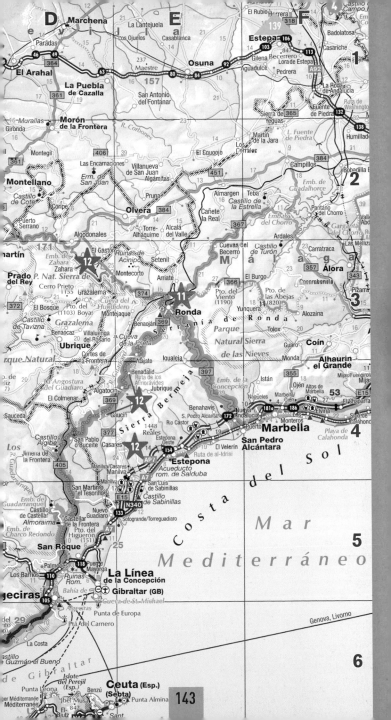

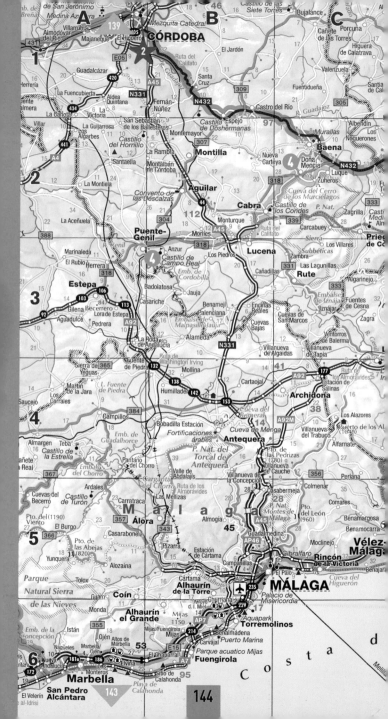

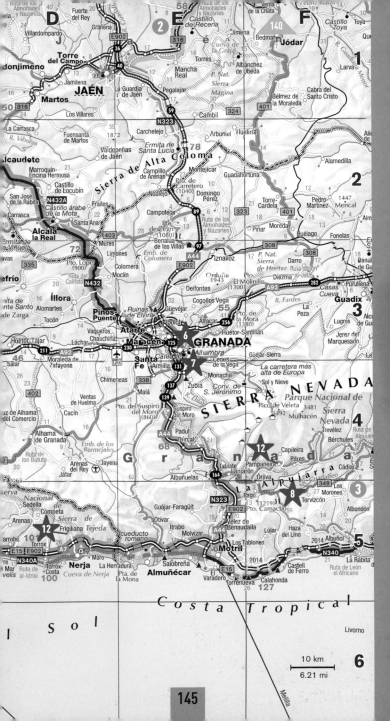

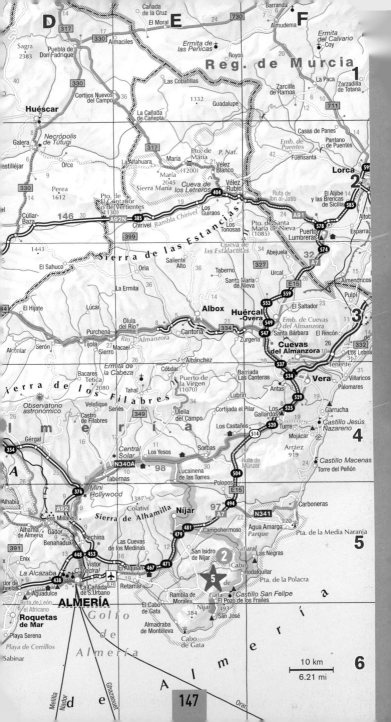

KEY TO ROAD ATLAS

Motorway with junctions
Autobahn mit Anschlussstellen

Motorway under construction
Autobahn in Bau

Toll station
Mautstelle

Roadside restaurant and hotel
Raststätte mit Übernachtung

Roadside restaurant
Raststätte

Filling-station
Tankstelle

Dual carriage-way with
motorway characteristics
with junction
Autobahnähnliche Schnell-
straße mit Anschlussstelle

Trunk road
Fernverkehrsstraße

Thoroughfare
Durchgangsstraße

Important main road
Wichtige Hauptstraße

Main road
Hauptstraße

Secondary road
Nebenstraße

Railway
Eisenbahn

Car-loading terminal
Autozug-Terminal

Mountain railway
Zahnradbahn

Aerial cableway
Kabinenschwebebahn

Railway ferry
Eisenbahnfähre

Car ferry
Autofähre

Shipping route
Schifffahrtslinie

Route with
beautiful scenery
Landschaftlich besonders
schöne Strecke

Alleenstr. Tourist route
Touristenstraße

XI-V Closure in winter
Wintersperre

Road closed to motor traffic
Straße für Kfz gesperrt

8% Important gradients
Bedeutende Steigungen

Not recommended
for caravans
Für Wohnwagen nicht
empfehlenswert

Closed for caravans
Für Wohnwagen gesperrt

Important panoramic view
Besonders schöner Ausblick

* Wartenstein Of interest: culture - nature
* Umbalfälle Sehenswert: Kultur - Natur

Bathing beach
Badestrand

National park, nature park
Nationalpark, Naturpark

Prohibited area
Sperrgebiet

Church
Kirche

Monastery
Kloster

Palace, castle
Schloss, Burg

Mosque
Moschee

Ruins
Ruinen

Lighthouse
Leuchtturm

Tower
Turm

Cave
Höhle

Archaeological excavation
Ausgrabungsstätte

Youth hostel
Jugendherberge

Isolated hotel
Allein stehendes Hotel

Refuge
Berghütte

Camping site
Campingplatz

Airport
Flughafen

Regional airport
Regionalflughafen

Airfield
Flugplatz

National boundary
Staatsgrenze

Administrative boundary
Verwaltungsgrenze

Check-point
Grenzkontrollstelle

Check-point with
restrictions
Grenzkontrollstelle mit
Beschränkung

ROMA Capital
Hauptstadt

VENÉZIA Seat of the administration
Verwaltungssitz

Trips & Tours
Ausflüge & Touren

The perfect route
Perfekte Route

1 MARCO POLO Highlight
MARCO POLO Highlight

INDEX

This index lists all cantons, places, mountains and destinations featured in this guide. Numbers in bold indicate a main entry.

WRITE TO US

e-mail: info@marcopologuides.co.uk

Did you have a great holiday?
Is there something on your mind?
Whatever it is, let us know!
Whether you want to praise, alert us
to errors or give us a personal tip –
MARCO POLO would be pleased to
hear from you.
We do everything we can to provide the
very latest information for your trip.

Nevertheless, despite all of our authors'
thorough research, errors can creep in.
MARCO POLO does not accept any
liability for this. Please contact us by
e-mail or post.

MARCO POLO Travel Publishing Ltd
Pinewood, Chineham Business Park
Crockford Lane, Chineham
Basingstoke, Hampshire RG24 8AL
United Kingdom

PICTURE CREDITS

On the cover: Sevilla, la Feria de Abril, Flamenco (Huber: Giovanni Simeone)
DuMont Bildarchiv: Gonzales (75, 118/119, 120 bottom); R. Gerth (37, 60, 62/63, 66/67, 69, 106/107, 127, 134/135); Huber: Giovanni Simeone (1 top); © istockphoto.com: Alija (16 centre); G. Jung (91); M. Kirchgessner (2 centre bottom, 20, 32/33, 42/43, 113); Laif: Tophoven (front flap right, 80), Zinn (40); K. Maeritz (3 bottom, 38/39, 85, 99, 110/111); mauritius images: Age (93), Alamy (2 centre top, 3 centre, 4, 7, 26 right, 30 left, 30 right, 44, 47, 70, 72/73, 78, 89, 104/105, 114/115, 120 top), Bridge (10/11, 149), Troisfontaines (8); Angel Perdomo (17 top); Purobeach Marbella (16 bottom); D. Renckhoff (2 top, 5, 21, 27, 28/29, 51, 57, 82, 108, 124); L. Schmidt (1 bottom); A. Selbach (6, 9, 121); O. Stadler (2 bottom, 3 top, 12/13, 58/59, 76/77, 96/97); T. P. Widmann (front flap left, 29, 94, 101, 103, 118); WAVE CULTURE: Stefan Strauss (17 bottom); White Star: Gumm (15, 18/19, 22, 24/25, 26 left, 28, 34, 48/49, 52, 55, 65, 87, 116, 119, 125); www.liliansimonsson.tv: Teteria Baraka (16 top)

1st Edition 2014
Worldwide Distribution: Marco Polo Travel Publishing Ltd, Pinewood, Chineham Business Park, Crockford Lane, Basingstoke, Hampshire RG24 8AL, United Kingdom. E-mail: sales@marcopolouk.com
© MAIRDUMONT GmbH & Co. KG, Ostfildern
Chief editor: Marion Zorn
Author: Martin Dahms, co-author: Lothar Schmidt; editor: Ann-Katrin Kutzner
Programme supervision: Ann-Katrin Kutzner, Nikolai Michaelis
Picture editors: Gabriele Forst
What's hot: wunder media, Munich
Cartography road atlas & pull-out map: © MAIRDUMONT, Ostfildern
Design: milchhof : atelier, Berlin; Front cover, pull-out map cover, page 1: factor product munich
Translated from German by Christopher Wynne; editor of the English edition: Sarah Trenker
Prepress: M. Feuerstein, Wigel
Phrase book in cooperation with Ernst Klett Sprachen GmbH, Stuttgart, Editorial by Pons Wörterbücher

DOS & DON'TS

When in Andalucía do as the Andalucíans do

DON'T AUTOMATICALLY SPEAK ENGLISH

The world is ours for the taking – well, that's what a lot of tourists think. They assume they can speak just like they do at home. English may a global language, but how about asking first – in Spanish: *¿Habla inglés?* The Spanish are not the best linguists and it always goes down well if you try to speak Spanish.

DO TAKE THINGS EASY

You may find the guy behind the counter at the post office or the woman at the car hire a bit on the slow side. But if you get hot under the collar that's not going to speed things up. You're on holiday, so relax, and do as the Spaniards do – change down a gear.

DON'T GET THINGS WRONG

A kiss on the cheek to the left and then to the right, and a wonderful smile – don't take things too personally, such welcomes are simply part of everyday life in Andalucía and have nothing to do with more complex emotions. Men, by the way, always shake hands.

DO RESPECT OTHER PEOPLE'S PRIVACY

The bar is packed – but there's just one Spaniard on his own at a table in the corner. Leave him alone – no Andalucían would ever even think of sitting down at a table with someone they don't know!

DON'T CLAP

Joining in the clapping during a flamenco dance is just about on a par with singing during an opera. *Palmas*, the rhythmic clapping of hands, is an integral part of the music and only those who are experts clap. Tablaos for tourists are an unfortunate exception.

DO DRESS PROPERLY

And don't wear sandals. Every country has it clichés but Spaniards know immediately who is a *guiri* – a tourist, mostly from northern Europe – from their poor taste in clothing.

DON'T HELP PICKPOCKETS

Andalucía is no more a problem zone than any other tourist area in Europe but there are always people ready to grab your wallet. Keep your eye on your valuables and carry your papers on your person rather than in a handbag. If you do have anything stolen, register it at the nearest police station or else your insurance will not pay.

DO BE WARY OF FLAMENCO RIP-OFFS

In some holiday resorts flamenco performances are often not very authentic and not worth the admission price. However, in Sevilla and Granada, for example, there are many artistically worthwhile performances by well-known flamenco dancers.